Tony's 50,000 Co-incidence Miracles

Anthony F. J. Coscia

En Route Books and Media, LLC
5705 Rhodes Avenue
St. Louis, MO 63109

Cover credit: TJ Burdick

LCCN: 2017950920

ISBN-10:0-9991143-7-9

ISBN-13:978-0-9991143-7-7

WELCOME TO...

Tony's 50,000 Co-incidence Miracles

Let me, **Anthony F. J. Coscia, author, teacher, evangelist, lecturer, and business professional, *CONVINCE you that God sends YOU MIRACLES ... every single day!***

Convincing stories: This book provides many true stories with evidence that we can all notice personal hourly-miracles if we just pay more attention to what is happening around us each day.

50,000 miracles so far: The author has experienced an average of three miracles per day for 50 years. This calculates out to 50,000 so far!

Trust the author: Tony wrote this book after God inspired him to write it and after 50 years of experiencing many miracles. Tony is very aware that he has a responsibility to convey God's Will carefully throughout this book.

Trust the flow of this book: Things are arranged in such a way so that you will grow more aware of the nature of the each miracle as you read along.

Here are some Bible Passages -- to convince us to notice our own daily "Co-incidence Miracles" from God:

John 14: ... Jesus said ... [12] truly, truly, I say to you, he who believes in me will also do the works that I do; and greater works than these will he do, because I go to the Father.

John 15: ... Jesus said ... [16] you did not choose me, but I chose you and appointed you that you should go and bear fruit and that your fruit should abide; so that whatever you ask the Father in my name, he may give it to you.

Mark.13: [11] And when they bring you to trial and deliver you up, do not be anxious beforehand what you are to say; but say whatever is given you in that hour, for it is not you who speak, but the Holy Spirit.

Mark.16: [20] and they went forth and preached everywhere, while the Lord worked with them and confirmed the message by the signs that attended it. Amen.

James.1: [5] if any of you lacks wisdom <u>let him ask God, who gives to all men generously</u> and without reproaching, and it will be given him.

Revelation.3: Jesus said ... [20] Behold, I stand at the door and knock; if any one hears my voice and opens the door, <u>I will come in to him and eat with him,</u> and he with me.

Psalm.54: [4] Behold, <u>God is my helper</u>; the Lord is the <u>upholder of my life</u>.

Psalm.96: [3] declare his glory among the nations, <u>his marvelous works</u> among all the peoples!

Matt.11: [28] <u>Come to me</u>, all who labor and are heavy laden, and <u>I will give you rest</u>.

<u>Summary of -- "Our Welcoming Letter":</u>

This book was written to achieve its main and important mission of helping people to notice and enjoy the many miracles which go un-noticed in our lives all day long (every day).

This mission alone helps people to become close personal friends of Jesus **very quickly** -- because each miracle is also a personal experience between God and each person. Therefore, as we notice each miracle, we also simultaneously notice that we are indeed co-existing with Jesus all day long. In fact, the miracles actually prove this to us in a powerful and convincing way; a way that was lovingly conceived and created by God. We become sure, positive, and confident of the friendship of Jesus because the miracles (the works alone) do convince us that Jesus is in fact and indeed (intentionally, voluntarily, and lovingly alive within each person's soul).

You will find the above mission of this book was wonderfully affirmed for all of us by the Blessed Virgin Mary on 08-02-2017 (ref. Exhibit-H).

And you will find that the above mission of this book was also wonderfully affirmed again by Jesus Himself if you refer to the Post-Script section which is mentioned at the end of Chapter 09.

I am honored, privileged, and humbled by the fact that Jesus has allowed me to participate with Him in producing this wonderful life-changing book. I can feel the great-love He has in His huge-heart for those He is reaching with this book.

May you enjoy your co-existence with Jesus from this day forward, forever!

Tony Coscia (a friend of Christ, by God's Grace).

<u>Some comments from readers to date:</u>

"I did read the first 4 chapters non-stop and I can't wait to get back to read chapter 5." **... FMM**

"You absolutely have to get this book out to as many people as possible, without delay!" **... FBM**

"It is amazing! I wish I knew about this process and these true stories years ago. I am already enjoying the process."
... AFC

"It seemed so simple and you explained the process so very well. I started noticing the Miracle-Clues you mentioned on the very next day." **... JAC**

"Wow! Really a great read. It was very impactful and convincing! I could not put it down once I began." **...
EJC**

"It was an experience! I never realized that we could live that way and see those things. I now realize that I have been missing many of my daily miracles. Thank you!" **... SAM**

Three miracles a day for fifty years averages out to 50,000 miracles . . . so far!

Our Lady of Medjugorje's message on 08-02-2017 did confirm the inspired mission of this book. Our Lady's message is included with a message from her Son Jesus Christ on Exhibit-H.

Brief and helpful notes to read before using this book

A ... Bible References: The Bible references in this book are from the "Revised Standard Version." Tony also recommends using:

1. "The Jerusalem Bible (annotated version)." Library of Congress Catalog Card Number 66-24278. Copyright at 1966 by Darton, Longman & Todd, Ltd.
2. "The New American Bible -- Revised Edition."

B ... Numbers used by Christian Authors: After you see the Table of Contents below; you can find Exhibit A, to read about the holy meaning and significance of numbers like 444 and 777 which are mentioned in this book.

For example: Bethlehem where Jesus was born and Golgotha where Jesus died; are both at 777-meters above sea level. The Jews also held (777) to be the holiest of numbers even centuries before Christ's birth.

C ... <u>Who is God?</u> – We may understand God differently, but there is still only ONE-God. He is "Our Ever-Present: Creator and Friend!"

Table of Contents

Tony's 50,000 Co-incidence Miracles

(This book will convince you that God sends EVERYONE miracles EVERY DAY)

E X H I B I T S

Page ... EXHIBIT ... TOPIC OR ITEM

Address and Contact
Anthony F. J. Coscia
P.O. Box 301
Willimantic, CT 06226
Emails to Tony: With777With@aol.com

DEDICATION OF THIS BOOK

<u>To Julie (Champagne) Coscia</u> ... my high school sweetheart who became my wife.

After 53 wonderful years of marriage, she peacefully passed into eternity at 4:44: AM while we were still holding hands. Fortunately, my heart is confident and sure that that she is now happy in heaven. She was a truly wonderful woman, mother, and wife – who always radiated "A unique and welcoming presence of Christ to everyone."

We always had really wonderful family gatherings and social events when Julie was here. She planned each event as if it was something like the coronation of a king ... and every event she planned was memorable. We never realized that the ambiance and personality of each event was really due to her actual living presence. She was so welcoming and she radiated joy to everyone who arrived, which always made everyone feel welcomed and special. Now that she has gone to heaven – we have not been able to replace her unique presence and personality. We all miss her presence among us.

As of our last count, we have been blessed with 5 grandchildren (Bailey, Bryan, Carolann, Gavin, and Liam) and 2-great grandchildren (Anthony and Bryan).

The miracles which surrounded her passing are explained in chapter 05. She had a unique relationship with Jesus and Mary and often made decisions with clarity and peace, telling me that God would take care of things. She was a great spiritual sounding board for me (a treasure to have in a wife). I often sensed God acting through her, and for me, in our 53 years of marriage. She was a piece of heaven on earth for me!

INTRODUCTION TO THIS BOOK

It is important to clarify some basic things about this book from the very beginning so that you can then enjoy using and referring to this book as you proceed to read it and use it in the future.

This introduction will allow you to often just open the book at random to read wherever God nudges and leads you to be open to (at random). In addition, this introduction will clarify the foundation from which I write so that you and I are partners: me writing what I believe God wants me to write ... and you understanding what you read, only and exactly how God wants you to understand it -- for your own personal walk with God each day.

After 50 years of witnessing thousands of miracles in my life, God has inspired me to write this book in order to help others to know God's Friendship and His Miracles too. Calculating 50-years at 3-miracles a day on average, calculates out to well over 50,000 miracles so far.

I am positive that it is impossible to be a friend of God and then to never notice a miracle (because everything God does is a miracle).

As I understand God's will for me at present, my purpose is to share some of these amazing moments in my life so that people who hear about these Godly-Co-Incidences and amazing unexplainable things in life ... might also come to notice these same things in their own lives too. God loves us with a flawless and powerful love – a love which can't help but gift-us and bless-us with miracles when we allow Him to co-exist and to live within and through us each day.

It is so amazing, and yet very simple that once we believe in God's constant love for each one of us, and then act in faith on that belief, God shows us that He is indeed really co-existing with each one of us.

Miracles do help to firmly convince-us of the truths of the bible. I mean, if we are trying to follow the teachings about God which are found in the bible, and in Tradition, and in His Church; then, we will automatically begin to notice miracles each day. <u>What other more-convincing evidence can there be than</u>

miracles? The bible is filled with miracles, and it is very doubtful that anyone would ever believe in God if they never heard about or actually experienced a miracle.

We actually do not befriend God ourselves. We only search for Him. Then, when God decides that we are sincere and honest in our search for Him, He personally empowers us to find Him and to become His friends.

We cannot create our friendship with God, nor do we create the miracles which we experience as His friends. It is God who advances us to the rank of "His-Friends" and who works all the miracles which we experience in our lives. As recipients of these great gifts (miracles), we become witnesses and encouragers to those around us; to encourage them to try to find God in their own lives too.

Even Noah, who built the ark before the great flood, was still only the recipient of the miracles which God created for him. And even the great and wonderful Moses was not himself the producer of the miracle which parted the Red Sea. Moses simply did God's will and God Himself parted the waters of the sea.

Accordingly, no one can boast of having any miracles of their own ... because all miracles are from and by God. Jesus said in John.16 [24]: "Hitherto you have asked nothing in my name; ask, and you will receive, that your joy may be full."

Now that you can review the Table of Contents and pick the miracles you wish to read about. I would still strongly urge you to read chapters 01 and 02 (even if you just only scan them quickly).

I was inspired by God to add these two chapters exactly where they are so that you will at least understand the process God uses in our lives to inspire us to see and to know His will in our lives. These two chapters have helped many people to better understand how to notice the many miracles which God sends to all of us every day. These two chapters will help you to understand the methods I used to notice God in the miracles which I write about in this book.

Mission ... This book has a mission:

I have come to learn that God truly loves us. We can see this in the fact that He made us and gave us all we need in order to exist and thrive. He made plants, food, water, oxygen, and many other things to support our lives and to help us to achieve happiness (as His friends).

I used to think that God was offended and saddened by the fact that many of the 7 billion people on earth never notice the miracles which God sends to every person (every day). I used to think that God must feel like He wraps gifts in boxes with pretty paper and ribbons for every person, every day – but hardly anyone notices that He sent the gifts.

But I talked to Jesus about this one day, and He inspired me to understand that I was only partially correct. He said that the fact that many people never notice His gifts are coming from Him each day does indeed sadden Him, but there is something that saddens Him more.

He sees the souls He has created to be His friends being

manipulated and tricked (just like Adam and Eve were), and He sees this trickery causing billons of souls to miss out on achieving their Heavenly reward.

God desires that people will stay in communication with Him every day so that He can guide them toward their best daily decisions. God also desires that this book will convince many to notice the daily signs and clues He is sending to each soul: "His daily co-incidence miracles."

Our Lady of Medjugorje's message on 08-02-2017 did confirm the inspired mission of this book. Our Lady's message is included on Exhibit-H.

This mission statement was also confirmed again by Jesus Himself just before we delivered the book to the printer -- and you can read about that final confirmation in the Summary and Conclusion section which is located at the end of this book.

About the author: Anthony Francis John Coscia (Tony)*

After 50-years of being blessed by Jesus in many miraculous ways, Tony has been inspired by Jesus to write a book to document some of the daily miracles he has been blessed to notice. Tony understands that God's reason for writing a book now, after all these years, is so that someone in the future may benefit from seeing how loving and how friendly God is to those who seek Him each day.

Tony explains, "Most people think of miracles in terms of "'earthshaking events.'" People imagine that a miracle must be something "FLABBERGASTING," like the case where God used Moses to part the waters of the Red Sea by raising his staff over the waters.

"However, miracles are clearly defined by Merriam-Webster's Dictionary as "An unusual or wonderful event that is believed to be caused by the power of God." By using this definition, we can each find many tiny-miracles in our lives which we personally KNOW are acts from God. For example, if we have a splitting headache and we ask God to please take it away, and it absolutely disappears in a split-second after we pray, some people will call that "just a tiny-co-incidence" – but not us, because we KNOW it is a miracle, just like the miracle of the parting-of-the-waters by God, with and through Moses.

Immediately after Tony typed the above example about "splitting headaches," he heard Father Spitzer on EWTN-TV explaining the same concept – and how there are no such things as tiny-coincidences where God is involved because everything God does is a miracle, and not just a coincidence. You will notice many cases in this book where as soon as Tony typed the sentence which you will be reading, he would get some affirmation or confirmation almost "instantaneously." You will find some of these highlighted for you in Exhibit-E at the end of the book.

Tony was married to his wonderful wife Julie (his high school sweetheart) for 53 years. His beloved Julie has passed on into eternity now, but Tony still feels her loving presence in his life each day. They gave birth to 3 wonderful children (Lisa, Eric, and Tanya). And, at last count, they have had 5-grandchildren, and 2-great-grandchildren.

Tony grew up in a very loving and supportive family and he attended Catholic Grammar schools. He attended evening classes at college for 11-years while also working as an accountant full-time each day in order to obtain his college degrees. Tony spent 35 years working in the accounting and finance areas with companies like Clairol Hair coloring, International Silver, Johnson and Johnson, Remington Electric Shavers, and Timex Watches and also moved on to become the president of four other companies as well. Tony explains that Jesus tutored him each day on what to do as a company president in these four companies, with amazing success. Because of God's daily tutoring-miracles, Tony was able to turn around many negative and unprofitable business activities and to help these companies to succeed.

For the past 15-years, Tony has managed a business consulting and business coaching firm which helps senior management to utilize the techniques which Tony has learned from God in his professional business career over the past 50 years.

Tony has attended well over 40 annual spiritual-retreat-weekends on a wide variety of Spiritual Teachings. For well over 40 years now, Tony has also taught CCD-Sunday-School and has also been an active lay evangelist. As an evangelist, Tony has been issuing weekly inspirational letters since 1980. These weekly letters report on both weekly inspirations from Jesus and weekly miracles. You can email **With777With@aol.com** to be added to this FREE weekly letter. Tony has also appeared on radio and television as an evangelist (Ref. Exhibit-C).

Tony is often heard saying: "All of my peace and joy and happiness come from the moments when I am participating with Jesus in doing God's Will." Tony also says that "Jesus wants to co-exist with each person every day (as a close friend); we were created by God because He decided that He really wanted us to be His Friends."

(*) Tony's full name -- also became a miracle, (ref. Exhibit-E, item # 4).

Chapter 01– Entering the Miracle-Zone ... (noticing your miracles)

Just as understanding and appreciating fine-music or fine-art does require something like a sixth-sense; so also does understanding and appreciating the friendship of God also require a special sense too. When God sees that we are truly seeking Him for Himself and not for some other ulterior motives ... God gives us the grace to find Him.

At some point in this process, God decides that we have convinced Him that we do want to be His friends ... and so ... God accepts us and empowers us to become His friends. (John, 1:12 in scripture even tells us that Jesus even empowers us to become Divine Children of God).

In this Friendship-Zone, we become mindful of God being present and living near us and with us during our normal daily activities. We also experience some sort of communication with God as well, which nudges and prompts us to do good, and not evil, during our daily walk with God. The Catholic *Catechism* calls this "The Voice of God in Our Conscience" as follows:

1. "CCC-1776 -- Deep within his conscience man discovers a law which he has not laid upon himself but which he must obey. Its voice, ever calling him to love and <u>to do what is good and to avoid evil ...</u> sounds in his heart <u>at the right moment</u>. For man has in his heart a law inscribed by God. . . . His conscience is man's most secret core and his sanctuary. (There he is alone with God <u>whose voice echoes in his depths</u>)."

2. "CCC-1777 -- Moral conscience, present at the heart of the person, enjoins him at the appropriate moment, to do good, and to avoid evil. <u>It also judges particular choices</u>, approving those that are good and denouncing those that are evil. It bears witness to the authority of truth in reference to the supreme Good to which the human person is drawn, and it welcomes the commandments. <u>(When he listens to his conscience</u>, the prudent man <u>can hear God speaking</u>)."

Once we have convinced God that we are sincerely

seeking to know Him with good and honest motives; He blesses us to be able to communicate with Him in the above ways. Then, once we begin to communicate with God and to follow His directions in our consciences, we also begin to notice God's actions and loving protections in our daily lives. We notice **God's miracles** as we proceed to fulfill His-Will each day.

The Sky Above the Clouds

Courtesy of Wikipedia

Chapter 02– The 3-Phases of having conversations with God ...

There are basically 3-different-phases in the process of talking with God. We may go from phase to phase, and back and forth during the day, depending on what topics and issues we are talking to God about.

Phase 01 – Talking (as if at the closet): ... Most people will admit that they talk to themselves on occasion. This seems most obvious when we are at the closet (getting dressed in the morning), or at the bureau selecting what to wear for the day. Most people will admit that they talk to themselves at the closet ... in ways similar to the following:

We ask ourselves things like .....

(1.) "I wonder if I should wear that red shirt with those blue pants."

<u>And then we answer ourselves</u> with something like ...

"No, I better not do that, because my boss told me that was a terrible and stupid match the last time I wore that combination."

<u>Or we ask ourselves</u> something like .....

(2.) "I wonder if that sports jacket will match those slacks and shoes."

<u>And then we answer ourselves</u> with something like ...

"Yes, that combination looks great together."

This can go on and on for a while each day, but my point is this: We are actually <u>asking ourselves questions</u> about what to wear as we dress up for the day (AND AS ASTONISHING AS IT MAY SEEM ... WE ARE (all of us) <u>ACTUALLY ANSWERING OURSELVES AS WELL</u>).

This same pattern also occurs when we are at the supermarket and purchasing groceries. We ask ourselves questions like "What price should I pay, or what size should I buy" ... and we answer ourselves here as well. We also talk to ourselves and answer ourselves in many other cases too, like: choosing books at the library, or in deciding what criteria to use when we search for info on the Internet, or when we are writing a letter or a book -- and we wonder if the words we are using are clear enough.

Jesus has taught me in my life that this process (talking as if we are at the closet) is a very natural part of all of us <u>because God did create this ability within us</u> – namely; <u>to ask Him for directions and to hear His replies</u>. We are even baptized as (Priests, Prophets, and Kings) when we are baptized, and we do then receive the gift of Prophecy, even at that early point in life when we are baptized as an infant. So, after baptism it is no surprise to me that we (even as infants), can indeed talk with God as the Catechism explains in the articles 1776 and 1777 above.

Jesus even showed me one day that I had been using this process as a little child long ago, even as I was playing in the sandbox as a tiny child. <u>For example:</u> Even as a tiny child. I would think and strategize about taking the shovel and bucket away from some other child in the sandbox so that I could use it instead of him or her. Again, Jesus was giving us the answers way back then too, as children. In my case, the voice of Jesus (which is the voice of our conscience) would nudge me to let the other boy keep the bucket and shovel or ask the boy if I could borrow it.

I now even realize that we are all asking and answering ourselves even in the crib as babies when we decide to YELL-LOUDER to get our diapers changed. See, this method is ACTIVE in us even before we learn to speak real words. I am convinced it is a spiritual gift from God and that after baptism we do have the voice of God active in our consciences – answering questions and guiding us, even though we may not realize who Jesus is until later in life.

Hopefully the following will convince you to use the above methods when you are talking with Jesus about the choices you make in life. I know that God has built us with this ability because some of my friends and I have been using this method for many years with wonderful results. The following confirms the reality of this method too:

1. <u>For example .... St. Paul said</u>: "We Have the mind of Christ (ref. 1-Corinthians, 2:16)"

2. **And Jesus said the following things**:

   <u>Luke.12</u> [12] for the Holy Spirit will teach you in that very hour what you ought to say.

   <u>John.14</u> [26] But the Counselor, the Holy Spirit, whom the Father will send in my name, he will teach you all things.

3. **And St. James said:**

   <u>James.-1</u> [5] if any of you lacks wisdom let him ask God, who gives to all men generously and without reproaching, and it will be given him. [6] But let him ask in faith, with no doubting, for he who doubts is like a wave of the sea that is driven and tossed by the wind.

Perhaps you have noticed in the above examples that (after being baptized as a prophet ... and standing at the closet door getting dressed in the morning); the voice which asks the question is YOUR VOICE ... and the voice which answers you is GOD LIVING WITHIN YOUR CONSCIENCE -- as the Catholic Catechism similarly explains in articles: CCC 1776 and 1777 above (which say: "conscience gives us the right choices").

Notice in the above closet and supermarket example --
that when we ask ourselves a question (it is because we
do not **YET** know what the answer is, <u>otherwise we
would not be asking a question</u>) ... so the fact that the
answer arrives immediately after we ask – implies that
the answer is not coming from <u>the same person who
asked the question.</u> (The person who asked the question
obviously did not know the answer when they asked the
question.) But the answer is, however, coming <u>from the
PERSON who knows all the answers -- namely; The
Presence of God dwelling within us, which begins at
baptism.</u>

**Phase 02 – (Discussing things face-to-face with
God): ...** In this second phase, we have already tried to
use THE CLOSET PHASE METHOD (Phase 01 above) --
but Jesus has responded to us with instructions (like
inspirations in our Conscience) which are difficult for us
to believe or accept without pondering them for a while.
Also, sometimes Jesus just wants to have a sit down
discussion with us because He wants to talk to us about
some things -- like two friends, face-to-face (the way He
did with Moses in the desert).

For example ... Jesus may have inspired us to do some

things that we have never done before, or things that we know we are not very good at doing. This may cause us to have to sit down and talk with Jesus in our Consciences (mind-to-mind with Jesus) and to have longer chats with Jesus than just the quick yes and no (question and answer method) that we use when we are talking at the closet.

In this phase-02 now ... we continue to talk with Jesus until Jesus, who knows how to handle us perfectly well, convinces us that we can begin with what He has asked us to do. This phase-02 is usually tied closely to cases where we have self-doubt about our ability or our resources and tools, etc. However, we can surely use this method whenever we are not satisfied in using phase-01 and have doubts about what we are hearing in our consciences (in the closet Phase-01-phase).

We also use this Phase-02 method when we want to talk to Jesus as a friend about something that we need clarification about. The Closet Phase-01 method is more like getting a QUICK and simple YES or NO about our questions. So Phase-02 works better when we need a longer and more detailed answer to our questions.

Phase 03 – (Fleecing -- if we are confused or doubtful) ... Please note: The word <u>Fleece</u> in the dictionary has a very negative meaning. I.e., it can mean: "to swindle and overcharge someone for something." However in Scriptural terms, FLEECING refers to what General Gideon did in the Bible -- in the book of Judges (chapters 6 through 9). Namely, General Gideon wanted to be sure he was hearing God correctly, so he asked God to please show him a sign that he (Gideon) was really hearing God correctly. And our loving, kind, and merciful friend (God) did allow Gideon to ask for clues and a sign. Please note however that Gideon was not testing God as the Scribes and Pharisees did by asking Jesus to work a sign (a miracle) to prove that Jesus was from God.

Gideon was not asking God to prove that He was God; Gideon was asking for a sign that he (Gideon) was really hearing precisely what God wanted Gideon to do. And God did honor Gideon's honest request for clues by allowing Gideon to use a soft-fluffy, Fleece-Blanket, as a signal.

Here is an over-simplified Bible-Fleecing Summary ... but I encourage everyone to read the beautiful story of General Gideon asking God to please give him a clue that he was hearing God correctly. The story of Gideon is explained at the end of this book (in Exhibit-B). HOWEVER – Basically, and very simply stated for now: General Gideon puts a fleece-blanket out on the field one night and asks God to please make just the blanket ONLY become wet with dew during the night. He asks God to not let any dew at all fall on the ground (just only on the blanket) ... in order to show Gideon that he has heard God correctly. Then, the next night, because Gideon begins to doubt still further, he pleads with God (very respectfully and honestly) to please do the opposite and make the Fleece-Blanket remain dry while all the earth became wet.

The above was a simple summary so that at least you know that the Bible-Fleecing method does exist. If you are at a point in trying to do God's will and you are struggling with a lot of doubts or conflicting thoughts ... you can look at ***Exhibit-B*** at the end of this book for a very detailed and clear way to do something like what General Gideon did in order to be more certain of God's-Will.

NOTE: I should stress here that FLEECING is

something we do when we do not have peace and clarity about doing God's will, even though we have already used the first two phases of talking to God, already discussed above. The reason we always use the first two phases of talking to God first (before asking for a fleece plan) is that God wants us to have faith and to get to know Him well enough so that we have "a good second nature feeling about when He is talking to us and guiding us." His voice sounds like our own normal voice which we hear in our thoughts each day. Remember: St Paul said: "We have the mind of Christ." (Ref. 1-Cor. 2:16)

The more often we talk to God about doing His will, the more we will become accustomed to the feeling of His-Presence and to the sound of His-Voice sounding in our hearts and minds. Eventually, we should not have to do any fleecing (because FLEECING is something we do when we are confused or doubtful about what we think God is saying). Certainly it is better to use FLEECING than to proceed in doubt. But remember to ask GOD to give you the fleecing methods to use (instead of you telling Him). God will give you the steps to use in your fleece if you ask Him to do so. This way, you will have the wisest-fleece possible (God's Fleece).

Chapter 03– God's Convincing Miracles...

God Himself makes us His friends when He decides that our desire to be His friend is honest and true. In addition, He Himself knows what sorts of convincing evidence we need to see in order for us to believe that He is talking to us every day. In St. Paul's case, God actually stunned St. Paul with a bright light and the powerful voice of God and then a period of actual total blindness before Ananias came to heal Paul of blindness. And, in the cases of the 12-apostles, Jesus curses a fig tree and calms a storm, and raises Lazarus from the dead (and performs many other miracles), in order to destroy their doubts and to increase their faith. In fact, it is highly doubtful that anyone would have been convinced of Jesus' divinity if there were not any miracles at all being witnessed and attributed to Jesus as He walked among us on Earth (both then and now as well). Just Google and then consider the miracles of Lourdes in 1857 and also the miracles in Fatima in 1917 as examples of current miracles. In addition, there have been over 200 actual documented apparitions of The Blessed Virgin Mary from 1975 through 2017 – and still continuing in Medjugorje (Yugoslavia) since 1981. Jesus has appeared to quite a few of the 8,000 saints who have lived among us over the past 2,000 years. One such case is the recent life story of St. Faustina in 1931. Ultimately, all God's clues are miracles!

Miracles in Crisis: I was 24 years old, and I had married my high school sweetheart five years earlier when I was 19 years old. I was currently suffering a lot of stress because we had just purchased a house, and I was working two jobs to try to pay all the bills. I was also attending college three evenings a week to get my bachelor's degree, and I had a job in accounting which was very demanding and stressful, and we had just given birth to our first child. Perhaps I am weaker than most people, but this was all a heavy stressful load for me personally at the time.

My life was a mess. I had little time to enjoy being married to a wonderful woman (Julie), and no time to enjoy my first child, and my bills were mounting to more than I could afford. I spent any spare time I had doing school homework in order to get good grades to graduate and to get a better job. Worse yet, although I was oblivious to it at the time, I was not going to church or praying or thinking of God at all -- ever.

I found each day bringing more and more fear of failure into my mind, and fear of losing a great wife, and fear of losing my job, and I was always sad, frustrated, and exhausted. I felt like I was always lacking any time: to relax, or talk to my wife, or play with my new born, or even sleep. Emotionally, I felt as if I was always mentally gasping for air all day long. I was always rushing to get everything and anything done.

It kept getting worse day by day until one day as I was passing by a very large Catholic Church, I suddenly realized that God inside could help me if He wanted to ... but I was angry that He was not helping me at all. Immediately, without much thought at all, and in a fit of desperation, I pulled over and parked right there in front of the church at a busy intersection and almost drove up on the curb in my haste and in my anger. Then, I stormed into the church and I told God off! Yes, I know this was stupid now ... but back then I felt as if I had nothing to lose, and I had no evidence that God really existed at that time in my life anyway. I was angry at everything and anything on this day!

Sadly – I was very rude and disrespectful to God (it was awful, and I am amazed I was not struck down by lightning). I said things like: "How do I know if you are really there; how does anyone really know? And if you are really there and you do see my sufferings, why are you not helping me? And, people say you are a loving and caring God ... but then, that can't be true -- if you are just watching me struggle and failing – and you do not help me at all. So, either you are not a loving and kind God ... or ... you really do not exist. You can't be BOTH: (on the one-hand; really loving and filled with kindness ... and then also simultaneously watching me suffer every day)! I also said ... all those nuns and priests you had me meet in my catholic school education must all be nuts, crazy, or stupid ... because they say you are there and you are loving and kind ... but you are not showing up to help me at all. And guess what, if you are really there – (and I really have no idea if you are right now) – then I am your problem (because you created me and you let me get into this mess, and I did not ask to be created and to live in this stressful nightmare). So whatever happens now is your problem, not mine. I did not make me, and I did not make you either – and I am giving up caring or even trying to care to ever try to be good anymore. Why bother!"

I said more things just as rude and disrespectful because I was there for well over an hour moaning and groaning. And then I left with a concluding remark ... "So ... If you are really there (and it sure does not look that way to me), then I am your problem ... I have done all I can do and I am failing and giving up. I do not even know if you are hearing me right now (so I am probably just talking to myself anyway) ... and how can anyone know really if you do care or if you do hear us at all when we cry out to you?"

So, I left the church and felt worse than before because if there really was a God ... I had probably just gotten Him very (VERY) angry. So I just destroyed any help I might have had (if He was real and He was there listening at all). So now I was sure that I was hopelessly lost for sure.

Strange, but something wonderful began to happen inside of me. I started having dreams about heaven and good dreams of pleasant things, and I felt loved by God - - (mainly because I was not getting any worse off each day, and He did not kill me in my sleep or strike me down with lightning after all I dumped on Him). I started reading small passages in the bible each night before bedtime (maybe only 3 or 4 lines of type), and I began to notice that God really had a lot of patience with some pretty bad people in the bible too. The bible seems to show Him as a loving and kind God, especially in the New Testament. I noticed that whenever God appears to be mean and angry (that it is only after He has had abundant patience and mercy for a very long time first). This gives me confidence in His-constant-Love whenever I approach Him now because I can see how in the bible He always starts with love (and remains that way for a very long time before people can cause Him to lose His patience). We have to be really bad (very bad) for God to get angry with us because He holds a perfect and powerful love for us which is very hard (almost impossible) for us to interfere with. We see a hint of His tremendous love just by looking at how He hung on a cross (as Jesus) so patiently and lovingly for us without getting angry, and then he looked at his torturers and said: "Father, forgive them; for they know not what they do"... (Ref. Luke 23:34).

Soon after this; I started to notice some miracles

happening in my life which began to convince me that God was very real after all. I would get ideas in prayer that seemed to come true ... and when I yelled from the deepest parts of my heart for HELP for understanding, I seemed to get it pretty quickly.

Then, not too long after I had told God off in anger – roughly about a month later -- I got a call from an executive-recruiter who said he could not reveal who gave him my name but that he had a job offer that paid me about 30% more than I was making (wow: that would solve a lot of stress for me). I went to an interview and I got the job on the spot at the very first interview.

Life began to get much better especially since I was actually experiencing miracles now almost daily. If we spend time with God and pay attention to Him, we can't help but notice the miracles that surround Him whenever <u>He moves, loves, thinks, wishes, or acts</u>.

I was finally seeing evidence of God ... so I no longer wondered if there was a God and if He loved me. And I began to enjoy going to daily morning mass -- (first to thank God for not destroying me in my angry ranting, and secondly for the great joy I now found in living with an awareness of His constant presence and His constant availability to us). I also owed Him a lot of thanks for the great new job and the great raise in pay too! I began to learn a lot about our great God at each morning mass, where the priest reads the bible and explains it to us daily. And, then, we even get to swallow The Holy Eucharistic bread.

The Forest Miracle: I had received a wonderful response from Our Great God -- whom I had mistreated and offended terribly with my stupid and rude attitude. And God had managed to still send me a miracle job (with a large raise) – where the recruiter mysteriously said he could not reveal his source on how he located me. I still wonder if an angel called the recruiter with my name, like the angel Raphael helped Tobias in the bible. (Ref. Tobit 3:17).

I had dropped my other part time job, and School was getting easier (or maybe I was getting smarter because of the wisdom God was granting me). I was actually doing well in handling courses like Accounting, Biology, and Law -- all in the same evening-division-semester.

And I started to do another thing; I started to go for a

walk in the nearby forest for about 15-minutes a day (near my job at lunchtime). I would walk and talk with God about things like the bible, which I had read just before bedtime the night before. And I would talk to God about the morning mass lectures (homilies), which the priests give at the daily morning mass. I was really enjoying attending each morning mass and learning a lot from the priest's lecture-homilies each morning.

I think I had been doing this for about a month in the same spot in the forest each day whenever I could do so (almost daily except when the boss needed me to take a shorter lunch during our busy periods).

.... And then it happened .... One day when I entered the forest to walk and talk with God (and after I had gotten a bit deeper into the forest) ... everything just stopped, and it suddenly got very quiet! I was standing still in a dead silence, and I felt as if I was surrounded by a vast and infinite presence of God who was everywhere – yes, everywhere, and even way beyond where I could see with my naked eyes! Everything had stopped -- like all of the noise of the forest just stopped! The wind in the trees, the birds chirping, and the sounds of the small animals like squirrels and rabbits and even all the insects – everything was very quiet!

This forest was next to a major highway too ... so the total stillness and quietness was impossible except that God was making it happen. I felt loved and cared for and in the presence of a huge powerful force which I sensed was just looking at me and studying me. The peace was very welcoming and comfortable; I never wanted to leave, but after about 5-minutes, it stopped and all the noise was back and it was time to go back to work after lunch.

I know I was changed in that time in the forest and I remember it every time I see the passage in the bible (in Genesis 28) where Jacob realized that He was in a similar forested place -- where Jacob just somehow KNEW God was there! Jacob called that place Bethel (translated as: "house of God"). I believe that, like Jacob, I too felt the presence of God in a forest that day. It was an unforgettable life-changing experience (granted by a very great and infinitely loving God).

This taught me to be more aware of God's-Vastness and what being in His Presence must feel like (although I am positive that I only experienced a tiny part of God's-

Presence and for a very short time). Nonetheless, it was both very powerful, and very peaceful, at the same time. I felt God's presence there (like what I imagine Jacob also felt).

This sensation-miracle and the earlier one about getting a new job with a 30% raise finally convinced me that God was indeed be-friending me and loving me. I was absolutely sure of that now for sure!

Here is what Jacob said in the bible when he felt God's Presence in the forest once too:

Genesis 28: **[17] And Jacob was afraid, and said, "How awesome is this place! This is none other than the house of God, and this is the gate of heaven."**

The "He-And-I" book: After a few years of growing closer to God and learning more and more about Him, I found I could talk to God and hear God too (like phase 01 and 02 explained earlier, above ... where I did explain: "the talking at the closet method"). But doubts also began to confuse me. I kept having the good experience of following what God told me to do in my job and in my daily routines, but some of my family and friends began to pull away from me as a Jesus-Freak to whom they did not want to talk unless they had to. Then, I believe the devil tried to derail me with a lot of doubts, especially whenever doing God's will at work did not always match what my boss wanted me to do.

So, like many others in history, I entered into a dry spell where I wondered if I was really hearing God speak to me in my heart and conscience, or if I was often just imagining a lot of these inspirations in my own head. I had not yet learned all about the three phases of talking to God which are explained in Chapter 02 above. I was still learning a lot about it at this point ... which I really did not fully understand yet. It seemed to work well and I thought that I was seeing good results from the CLOSET-TALKING-METHOD. And I had gotten a lot of wisdom by talking to God often, but sometimes I would wonder if it was only my imagination. I thought: "Maybe I was only talking to myself when I THOUGHT I was talking to God?" That is how the devil has been killing the faith of believers ever since the very beginning (with doubts)! He even tricked Adam and Eve (to doubt God's words in The Garden of Eden).

So after a long period of doubting, I began to doubt God

was really talking to me at all. Sometimes, it would be clear that God was talking to me because of the results (miracles) which would show up in a few minutes or in an hour. But if the results took a few days to occur, well, then, I would begin to doubt it was God's Voice.

Then, because of the doubts, I got sluggish and I stopped seeking directions and messages from God (and that is the beginning of the end for a life with God). Faith disappears when we stop trying to seek for His directions in our life. If we stop talking to God, we slowly begin to forget He is there (another devil trick is to keep us from talking to God).

I am told that many of the saints in history had these DOUBTFUL moments in their lives too. It seems this is a time where God tests us and shows us how weak our faith really is (so that, once we see our weakness, He can then help us to grow stronger). God gets our attention during this testing phase by showing us that we can't overcome evil and the devil's tricks without God's help. I find that when these doubting and testing phases come to us in life that we need to keep asking Jesus to please help us to unravel what is going on – and He always does clarify things for us if we do that. In the end, after we get through this testing-phase, we find our faith in Jesus is stronger than it ever was before.

Well, one winter night while I was still struggling with this doubting-phase of my life at about 7 PM and while I was co-hosting a birthday party with my wife for our son and his Cub-Scout-Group ... I sensed Jesus nudging me to leave the house and drive off to a local church about 4-miles away – Jesus wanted me to come and speak with Him and it felt pretty clear that He wanted me to come (right now!).

I began to use the # 02 level phase of talking to God by this time and so I said: "Dear Jesus ... the church is always locked up by 3 PM each day and I know that." But His inner-voice got very convincing, although still kind, gentle, and non-threatening. I felt Jesus wanted me to come to the church for some reason and it felt like a friend was saying: "Please come now!"

So I sheepishly went to my wife to explain (imagining that she would say she needed me to help with the 5-young cub scouts who were about to finish eating their cake just now). Fortunately for me, I had married a saint. She looked at me for a moment with a very loving and understanding look and she simply said: "Okay, Tony, go ahead; that is not a problem, I am doing okay." My wife Julie was a saint and a great blessing from God in my life! And she had great faith in sensing God's Will for her and us in ways that differed from mine, but when she sensed that God was telling her things she was always right about it.

So off I went now to a church, which, by the way, I still knew they locked up at 3 PM every day ... a point I kept reminding myself of as I drove the 4-miles it took to get there. And, yes, my state of doubting that I was hearing Jesus was getting worse as I drove over.

Somehow, I began to realize that this whole event was going to be a great test of God tonight (<u>a test which I did not manufacture</u>). I had been given a beckoning-message from God -- which I was just about to prove or disprove. What I mean is that now, if the church was all locked up, then that proved He was not calling me. Indeed, this was going to be a good test because if God was calling me to the church, then the church would be un-locked and there would be something happening there to confirm that Jesus did in fact want me to show up there tonight. So now I realized this was a very good test (but set up by God, not by me). Ps: my realization was really: "<u>God is inspiring me to KNOW.</u>"

So when I got to the church and got out of my car (in a very dark parking lot), and I pulled on the main door of the church (and found it was locked); I was extremely annoyed. I felt stupid that I drove over in the first place, and I felt that I just proved that indeed Jesus was NOT talking to me at all (ever). Boy was I angry and sure now that God had never talked to me at all in all those years where I really thought it was God. I felt like a jerk that had been stupidly imagining things for a very long time! I felt those people who did not believe my faith were right!

As I angrily walked back to my car ... I heard that same Jesus-voice saying: "But you have not tried all the doors yet to see if there is just possibly one door open." I thought; "Are you kidding?" There were 6-doors around a very large church building, and it was very dark. And I could see the priest's residence next door, so I wondered if they would call the police if they saw me poking around at this late hour. I surely did not want to tell a priest that Jesus told me to come here (so that the priest had to come and open up the door for me right-now)!

Now, I realized that if I did not check all the doors personally, I would never be sure if I was called here to this church tonight or not. I mean, if all the doors were locked, then Jesus could not have really called me to visit Him here, and that would prove that I was not hearing His Voice the way the catechism says we can (CCC # 1777).

So I did go around to all the doors -- and door after door I got more and more annoyed and hopeless. I reached the final door which was like a door used to toss packages inside ... it was never really used by anyone I knew at that church because it was a very small door. I grabbed the door handle and pulled real hard in anger and frustration because I reasoned that all those past wonderful moments where I thought God was talking to me were apparently, really just only my imagination. Because all the doors so far were locked up, I was sad and felt stupid and wondered: -- "How did I let all of this confusion happen to me? I was successful in my job and I had graduated college with good grades ... and here I am just a jerk after all, anyway!"

So fully expecting that this last door was also locked, I pulled the door handle really hard and fast in anger.

However, the door was not locked and I almost knocked my nose off. I pulled the door knob so hard and fast – and, I did not get my nose out of the way. All of my feelings of frustration and sadness, combined with the darkness and the cold night, all came together at that last door (door number 6 now) and caused me to pull it hard – because I was tired and frustrated and cold.

The next thing I noticed was that I was inside the church ... and the door made an awful slamming sound as if I was in a metal drum and a metal door had just slammed shut. It all happened so quickly that one minute I was outside, and suddenly, now I was inside ... and I did not really notice the transition. I think perhaps that I must have just jumped inside when the door opened (like I was accustomed to doing on the train and subway each day in New York City when those doors opened there too).

Anyway, I was inside now and the door slammed shut, and I heard something moving around in this <u>very ... very ... dark church</u>. I had no idea what was moving, but it sounded like something or someone rushing away from me as I had just suddenly landed inside. I froze there for a moment wondering if I should move at all.

Then, after what seemed to be a very long time of me being frozen there in fear, I began to quietly reach for and feel for the light switch ... which took a real long time to find in this deep darkness. Then finally with my hand on the light-switch, I began to focus my eyes (so I would be ready to see whatever I could see quickly -- and as soon as I turned on the lights). I figured that I might have to move really fast as soon as I turned on the lights because then I would see what had rushed away from me as I had entered the Church. I was like an athlete at the starting line of a race: ready to turn on the lights, and then immediately decide to run, or jump, or drop and roll (immediately), and just as soon as I turned on the lights. I had to be ready to react quickly as soon as I turned on the lights.

So I got myself ready to act quickly! I trained my eyes to be focused on the darkness but to look straight ahead in the direction of the noise which I had heard in that space earlier. Now I was ready to see whatever it was that moved, as soon as I turned on the light switch.

I took a deep breath, and I flipped the light switch on and the darkness was gone. And now, right in front of my nose was a book-rack with only one book on the top shelf – directly where my eyes were trained to watch for any activity. Nothing else was moving ... and then ... that same quiet voice of Jesus which I was used to hearing by now, said: "Take the book and look at it."

I do not know why, but I did not doubt that voice at that moment at all ... the voice was familiar, peaceful, polite, and somehow very convincing. So I took the book in my hands to open it up at random to see what I might see. I opened it at random and my eyes immediately noticed one line in the middle of the page which I had just opened to – and that line stated: <u>Jesus said: "Why do you doubt that you hear My voice ... don't you realize that I talk to all of my creatures?"</u>

I had opened that book at random (something had directed my two thumb-nails to that exact page). The book's title was (HE AND I). It was a true story and a diary of Gabrielle Bossis, a female actress in Europe in the 1940's. In her book, she lists her daily conversations with Jesus and on this very page; Jesus was asking her: "Why do you doubt my voice?"

The whole experience from start to finish was like a Hollywood Script: I was in a dark church ... I had six doors to check and only the last one was open ... and the book was there in front of my nose as I turned on the lights ... then; I open it at random to the page that says: "Why do you doubt that you hear my voice." WOW! I was absolutely convinced at that moment, that Jesus is absolutely my friend and my God too. He has taught me since then that: He does talk to – "all of us" – hourly ... as the catechism states in articles: CCC-1776 + CCC 1777. (Ref. Exhibit-G).

The New Heart Miracle: Jesus woke me from a sound sleep at 3 o'clock in the morning and inspired me to get up and go downstairs to the kitchen and write a letter to a man who was having heart surgery in the morning. The man was a close relative, and my wife would be going to visit him in the morning, but I could not be there until later in the day. I asked Jesus if I could wait until later since if I get up at 3 AM I will probably never fall back to sleep.

Funny, Jesus lovingly convinced me to go do it now for some reason. So I rolled over and got up and went down into the kitchen. My wife and three children were sound asleep.

I asked Jesus to inspire me with what to write. And Jesus nudged and prompted me (as if I was at the closet asking for advice in the morning – Like a phase-01 discussion explained earlier). Jesus inspired me to write some of what it says in Psalm-51 (i.e.; Create in me a New Heart, O Lord). Well, that made a lot of sense because the man was going to have heart surgery that very morning. So I began to write, intending to write something like:

"I am praying for you and praying that God will <u>create a brand new heart</u> for you during surgery later today, so that you will be stronger and better than ever by the end of this day" ....

... BUT ... Just as I wrote the words; "<u>create a brand new heart</u>" ... I heard the record-player in the living room go on ... and I heard the record drop into place on the turntable ... and then I heard the turntable begin to turn (swoosh, swoosh, swoosh), and I heard the arm with the needle settle on the record being played ... (and then I heard the most wonderful words being sung ... which were as follows: "<u>Create in me a new heart O Lord</u>"). WOW! ... The record was singing the same exact words which I had just written down! ... WOW! You see, we had such a record which we listened to often – where the vocalist sings the words to Psalm-51 ... (CREATE A NEW HEART IN ME O' GOD).

I immediately got up to check and see who had played this trick on me and put that record on while I was writing the exact same words in the kitchen. But, as I went to check, Jesus made me realize that nobody but He alone would know my thoughts at 3 AM. I did check though and did find all 3- kids were asleep and my wife was as well ... so I felt the clear and wonderful (amazing) presence of God with me there in this truly spectacular moment in life. I felt that same peaceful presence of God which I had experienced in the forest earlier (as explained above in the Forrest miracle).

The heart surgery was a great success and the man lived for another 13 years. Thank You Jesus!

The Marble Slab Miracle: I was out of work for about 18-months, and I was following all the great advice of the experts from Outplacement Firms who tutor job seekers on what to do ... and yet I was not getting any job offers. I was spending a lot of time visiting Jesus in the church before and after my job interviews (praying) and I got to know Jesus pretty well in that time of closeness and dependency on Him.

One day, as I was inside a Catholic church asking God what I did well, or not well, at a recent job interview (and what was to become of me and my family if I did not land a job soon), I felt His loving assurance that He was going to make it all work out and that I needed to trust Him more. Then, as I was walking down the side aisle of the church ... His inner voice spoke to me (His inner voice which is alive in our consciences as the catechism article number: CCC-1777 already explained above). Jesus said: "Sit here."

I looked down at "the seat" -- which Jesus meant, but it was only a half of a seat, and at the very end of a pew (you know, that place where the pew meets the very high marble stone pillars which hold up the roof, so that carpenters have to cut half of the seat off, in order to allow people to slide in and out of the pew as they squeeze by the stone pillar). I marveled at why Jesus wanted me to sit there with my knees touching the marble pillar and I jokingly told Jesus that; "I hoped nobody would come in and see me crunched here in this tiny space with my knees touching the pillar because they would certainly think I was very strange and maybe even think that I was NUTS too!" This was a very large church, and there were many more wonderful places to sit than crunched here -- balanced on ½ of a seat – facing a marble pillar! I was certainly thinking, as the bible says, "God's ways are not our ways."

Then Jesus said ... "LOOK." So, I looked at what I could, but the only thing that made sense was to look at the marble slab in front of my nose, which was also touching my knees. And, I was "astonished!" Right there in front of my nose was a marble slab with the curvy-lines of the usual marble-grain-work which is normally seen in marble. But these curvy-lines formed a picture (a painting – painted by God), who had formed this marble slab in some mountain, someplace, over some period of perhaps 5,000 years).

I realized that; when marble is cut and quarried from mountains of stone that the marble stone grains have been formed by centuries of fallen dead trees, and rain, mud, and soot, all being compressed under great pressure for centuries – compressed in order to form marble grain-lines in the stone. It has to be a miracle that people actually do cut a slab of marble and create a drawing too. The drawing itself has to be understood as a creative miracle because God arranged for the grain lines to form over many centuries of pressure under the earth, and then God guided the sawing equipment and the hands of the artisans who did cut the slab at which I was looking.

Jesus also inspired me to realize that during the quarrying process of creating slabs of marble, the position of the slicing and cutting equipment really determines what drawing we will see on the marble slab later on. If the cutting is only off by 1/64th of an inch (higher or lower on the mountaintop), it produces a totally different picture on the slab of marble which we ultimately see. So, God somehow also had to guide the hands of those people who were cutting the slabs of marble in order for this particular slab to depict the artwork God intended for us to see in the end.

What I saw very clearly was a painting (painted with God's marble grain-markings). The Godly-Painting was a painting of The Blessed Virgin Mary riding on a horse with St. Joseph her spouse walking alongside – and with the baby Jesus, lying across Mary's lap on his stomach. This slab of marble conveyed a clear picture of the actual time where The Holy Family left Israel for Egypt, during the time when King Herod was out killing all of the male children born during the time of the Magi visit as follows:

> **Matt.2**: [13] Now when they had departed, behold, an angel of the Lord appeared to Joseph in a dream and said, "Rise, take the child and his mother, and flee to Egypt, and remain there till I tell you; for Herod is about to search for the child, to destroy him."

Well, I was stunned of course, but I was made certain in that moment that Jesus truly loved me (because He had just granted me this "private viewing of His art work in marble"). My fears about getting a job were completely destroyed because I remembered that Jesus had told me a few minutes earlier not to worry, because He was going to make the job situation work out for me soon ... and now this Marble-Miracle arrived to remind and assure me that Jesus had always been a wonderful loving friend to me and pulled me through a lot of problems already I life.

I have taken many people to this church to view this

wonderful art-work whenever Jesus nudged me to do so -- and I have shown it to the pastor and to the sexton at the church too. The pastor wisely asked me not to publicize the whereabouts of the marble drawing because of the commotions or break-ins that this might cause. I do have a picture of the art work however to show to interested spirit-filled-souls when they ask for it. **Thank You Jesus for this amazing gift and memory !**

Please see exhibit (i) in the exhibit section of this book for the photo of the marble slab -- and for a tracing of the marble grain lines, which helps us to see the art-work of God a bit more easily (after seeing the tracing).

====================================

The Franciscan University of Steubenville (Prophecy Miracle): I was very blessed to be able to attend a total of 4-weeks of an intensive Bible-Study-Program at this Ohio University during the summers of 1979 and 1980. There were 500 to 700 attendees from all over the globe there in attendance, and I got to meet Father Mike Scanlan (a giant in the faith and the President of the university at the time). I met friends of

Jesus (real modern friends of Jesus -- with the same great faith of the apostles of old) who all came to this Bible-Study event to learn more about God at these conferences. They came from practically everywhere, and I personally met some wonderful people from Australia, Canada, Europe, and The United Kingdom.

During one day in the final days of the conference, while we were studying The ACTS of The Apostles section of the bible, the leaders asked us to form some groups out in the grassy areas of the University and to have some group-discussions about what we were studying in the "ACTS of the Apostles." Many different groups of people were formed to discuss the gifts of The Holy Spirit which the apostles had received and internalized 2,000 years ago (after the first Pentecost). Quite amazingly, 2,000 years ago, tongues of fire had appeared over the heads of the disciples as evidence that the Holy Spirit of God was baptizing them and filling them with many spiritual gifts. The bible verse stating this follows:

> **Acts.2:** [3] and there appeared to them tongues as of fire, distributed and resting on each one of them.

There were many groups formed in the grassy areas of the land mass there at Steubenville, and each group posted "discussion-topic-signs" attached to 6-foot-high poles, so we could walk along and visit with many different group discussion teams if we wanted to.

I found a small group of 7 people to join, which seemed comfortable and right for me, because I did want to understand their topic of <u>Prophecy</u> a bit more now; especially since I was hearing Christ's Voice in my conscience ... guiding me and loving me as a friend each day. I felt I still had a lot to learn. So I felt really blessed to find a small non-threatening-group to meet with.

The 8 of us began to chat and we all had questions and miracles in our lives to share ... but none of us had any clear answers on some key points. So, we all agreed to take the next 24-hours and to make a real effort to take notes of any and all inspirations or ideas or clarifications which we might get from Jesus over the next 24-hours, and then to meet again to compare notes, at this same hour on the next day.

On the next day when we met, each person began to take turns to tell us what they were blessed by Jesus to understand or ponder over the past 24-hours. As each person began to share, we quickly noticed that Jesus had given the same answers and same evidential-scriptures and ideas to several of us so that it was abundantly clear that Jesus had blessed every one of us with the same-wisdom about the same-topics over the past 24-hours. And now on this second day, Jesus was having us confirm the same messages which we had received separately, by being able to speak about them all together with each other. This was Prophesy at its best because we had instant confirmations right here from all of us, confirmations that Jesus had been tutoring each one of us for a long time and that today; He had brought us together from all over the globe to meet on this wonderful day together at Steubenville, Ohio.

I was the last person to share my list, but I had the benefit of listening to everyone else first. So, when it was my turn to share my list, I had tears rolling down my face because my full page list of about 15 items matched what everyone else had already shared. All I had to say was that I was given a stupendous gift to finally see confirmations which I had been craving to experience for several years now. Finally, after many years, I met people who were also experiencing the same sorts of things that I was. This was a great and perfect confirmation for me!

Many of you reading all this now probably knew long before I did that when we are Baptized, we are all blessed and named and called "priests, prophets, and kings." This means that we are all made prophets from the day of our own baptism. And by this baptismal gift, we are thereafter are able to hear the voice of God so that we can speak whatever He tells us to say (both to others on occasion ... and most often to ourselves). This is why we can have those discussions with God which appear to work just like the discussions we have at the closet in the morning and at the supermarket or the library, wherein God tells us interiorly which items to choose or to reject in our lives.

I hope you all have people in your lives who you can speak with about the spiritual events in your lives. When we do speak to others, we can get these same kinds of confirmations from each other because The Holy Spirit of Jesus does co-exist within all baptized Christians, and He can confirm and strengthen all of us when we meet together as brothers and sisters and talk about what He is teaching each one of us individually. Basically, when we meet together and talk about Jesus, Jesus speaks back to each of us from within others and ourselves too.

Attending a Catholic Charismatic Prayer Meeting is a really excellent way for us to experience these group-confirmations. Allowing Jesus to speak to us (from His presence within the people around us on a regular weekly or monthly basis) is really very beneficial to our spiritual growth. Ideally, if you have a spouse who shares your spirituality, you are truly blessed to be linked in such a way (which is the way that God intended us to be linked when God formed the team of ADAM and EVE and GOD).

The Church Piano Miracle: I was praying in an empty church before attending a meeting with one of my regular business clients and I was seeking wisdom about some of the things I was planning to say and do at the client's office. Then, just as I was about to leave the church and go to the meeting, I passed by the church piano and Jesus said in my soul ... "Look at the piano."

From where I was standing at that moment, I was in a perfect spot to see a very clear image of a life-sized face of Christ appearing on the side-panel of the piano (formed by the grains of the wood ... just like the grains in the marble had drawn a wonderful painting for God as explained in the Marble Pillar Miracle earlier in this book).

I was standing precisely in the perfect spot to see (God's piano painting) ... because the sun was shining in from the left side of the church and hitting the piano as if it was a spotlight ... and ... if I moved to the left or the right by 2-inches the "artwork of God was not as clearly visible." So, God had gotten me to stop and look as I was standing in the exact perfect spot to be able to experience this -- His-Piano-Grain-Painting.

I have told many people about this and shown it to many people as well. The pastor and sexton and parish secretary were greatly touched by the whole experience too ... and one man offered to buy the piano for a healthy sum of money. I guess it is no surprise that God is an artist (after all, we often properly call God, "The Creator of All Things").

The Locked School Miracle: I was part of a Cursillo Team giving a men's retreat weekend to a group of about 20-retreatants. We had been meeting for about 9-weeks as a team (consisting of about 20-men on the team). And we agreed to review the whole retreat plan on this scheduled night at a parish school building in our area of Connecticut. It was important that we all meet together, and we had a tough time getting everyone to agree on the date and time. In addition, if we did not meet on this night; it was doubtful we could hold a similar meeting in enough time before the actual weekend would be upon us. It was almost as if we had planned a coronation for a king and we were not sure yet if we all had our scripts correctly done and ready for each member of our team. We needed to be ready to handle everything well and like clockwork, so this rehearsal meeting really needed to be done on this night.

The 20 of us arrived for the final review, but nobody remembered to get the keys to the building. So, everyone began to rush around like ants on an ant-hill trying to find an open door or window to help us gain access to the school building.

I too, felt the pain of this shock just like everyone else, but Jesus clearly told me to stand still and remain where

I was standing while everyone else was rushing around trying to find an open door or window. I tried to move to some less obvious spot because the other 19-teammates were rushing around and it was getting dark ... and some of them looked at me in a judgmental way as if I was abandoning them in this moment of need because I was not moving at all. I really felt clearly that Jesus wanted me to stand there and to keep praying for them to find a way in – but Jesus wanted me to stand there in the open, in full view of everyone (which got a bit embarrassing too).

Talk about faith and trust in God ... Jesus had me standing out in the parking lot, very conspicuously on display ... so that every single person on the team saw me standing there and some made comments as they passed by me in their search. I only understood much later why Jesus wanted me conspicuously standing there and telling others: "it will be okay, Jesus will solve it."

Unfortunately, everyone gave up and started to congregate to agree on what to do because we couldn't get inside. And just then Jesus spoke in my soul and said ... "Tony: Go around to the right side of the building and open the door on that side of the building."

I knew it was the same voice that I had become familiar with over several years, so there was no denying it. But I did already see many men already run along that side of the building several times earlier, so, I was thinking that I must be misunderstanding Jesus because at least 5-men had already checked that side of the building as I watched earlier.

Jesus would not let go though ... He got me to notice His voice more and more and some of the team were talking about canceling the meeting. I felt that if I did not do as Jesus said to do right now – the cancelation was going to be my fault. So, I asked the men to wait a minute as I was going to check the right side of the building.

As I began to walk toward the building (boys will be boys you know) ... several men began to laugh and kid with me saying things like (Tony: we did that already) ... (Tony: where were you when we needed you). (Tony: you are a bit late buddy). Gosh! It was hard to hear all of those wise-crack-comments, but I felt that Jesus was happy with me for doing as He had told me to do, and that really helped me to overcome and cope with all the joking and negative comments for a few minutes.

Well, I got to the door on the side of the building and pulled it (even as some of the team was still laughing and joking), but the door did open. I was just as surprised as anyone else was!

Several men asked me in a joking way, what I did to open the door, asking things like: are you a safe-cracker, or a spy, or a gangster? ... But all Jesus told me to say was the truth. I said: ... "I felt Jesus say the door was open ... so I went and opened it."

Ps.121.8: The LORD will keep your going out ... and ... your coming in from this time forth, and for evermore. - Mark.16: [20] ... and they went forth and preached everywhere, while the Lord worked with them and confirmed the message by the signs that attended it.

Chapter 04– Miracles in Business …

I have been a business consultant and business coach for the past 15-years and God has helped me to help many key managers in business to rely on God's inner voice to improve their businesses with His guidance. The following are some miracles which occurred both while I was consulting and also while I was previously an employee in corporate America. My intention here is to glorify God and to convince any business people who might read this book that they can totally rely on God's inner-voice and guidance in managing their business affairs every single day. I have experienced many miracles which did save many companies from bankruptcy, all because I had asked Jesus to inspire us with solutions to some very difficult business decisions.

I have come to understand that God sees our businesses as little communities of people (much like tribes or as nations with a leader). Accordingly, God willingly works through and with leaders of businesses in order to bless them (and thus also to bless their employees by the blessings which He gives to the business leaders who trust God). God's many loving and wise blessings of a business are intended to bless the employees as well – just as He also blesses a nation through its God-loving-leaders (so that the citizens can benefit from the blessings too).

Client Box Story-01: I went to meet with a client president whom I had already been meeting with for well over 3 years. We had planned to meet on that Monday morning to review the company's profitability reports in order to see if we could prayerfully come up with some ideas to improve profits.

When I arrived on Monday, I found the president's office (which was normally very well-kept and tidy) now messy and cluttered with about 50-storage-boxes and with a lot of papers scattered: all over his office, on his chairs, and all over the floor. The employees told me that the company president had spent the whole weekend there at the office because he was told by his lawyer on Friday that he was being sued for a very large amount and he was therefore naturally very anxious and stressed-out. He needed to find the original copy of a specific contract in order to stop the lawsuit.

I began to feel very compassionate and concerned for the client. I have learned that true compassion becomes a great heart-felt-prayer inside of us when we really care for someone and want to relieve their problems. I began to mentally ask Jesus to help the man and to help me to be helpful as well. Immediately after asking Jesus to help me, I heard the voice of Christ in my soul and conscience telling me to look down next to my leg, and to take the yellow folder out of the box. There were about 15 folders in the box next to my leg, and only one of them was a yellow folder. I took the yellow folder out of the box, I opened it up, and there it was -- the original copy of the contract – sitting right on the very top of the documents in that folder. It was truly amazing and surely the inner voice of Christ had helped us.

What amazed me most was that Jesus had somehow gotten me to stand right next to the correct box out of the 50-boxes spread all throughout the president's office. It made me realize that God had already orchestrated where the boxes were being opened and where they were being set down on the floor (and this placement was apparently happening all throughout the long stressful weekend of the president's searching for the contract). God obviously knew that He was going to get me to be standing precisely and exactly in this correct spot on Monday morning. God had pre-set the stage and the scene.

I often notice in some of the miracles which I experience, that God has orchestrated things beforehand in order that things are pretty precisely arranged -- as if God was directing a play or a movie. We who do try to serve Jesus are something like actors in a play or a movie who do not realize how very precisely all the props in the movie are all carefully placed there by the movie director and crew, to be exactly where they will be needed in the moment of need. After 50 years of seeing such clues, I have become convinced that God is totally and lovingly involved and interested in even the smallest details of our daily and hourly lives.

Client Box Story-02: Ten years after the Client Box Story-01 above, I had another client who was trying to resolve a different legal issue and who asked me for some advice. I prayed for wisdom and made some suggestions for them to solve their particular issue.

Then about two weeks later, this second client met me and thanked me for my advice and told me that their problem was solved in a miraculous way. They told me that in order to solve their problem, they needed to find a legal document to prove a certain fact to some lawyers. Then, they surprised me with some amazing news when they said:

"You know, as I began to look for the legal document, it became necessary for me to go into the client's warehouse and rummage through about 70 filing-boxes. So I decided to do what you do and ask God for an inspiration to pick the right box to look in before I began to open all the boxes. And to my amazement, the very first box I opened contained all the legal documents that I needed."

How amazing this was – that I just met a client who had the exact same box-miracle as I did, but 10-years after I had experienced the same thing. How wonderful it is that we can always ask God for help with our business problems each day. And Jesus was so good to me to let me know that this second client also got to pick the correct box in their client box story-02.

And this just in! Client-Box-Story-02 happened about 12-months ago. However, just today (on 4-11-17) after I had just finished typing the above part of this book – Jesus arranged for me to providentially cross paths with this client. I was so amazed to see the client just after I had typed the above. I told the client that I had just typed the story about the 17-boxes ... and the client said: "No, not 17 ... it was 70-boxes."

How amazing this miracle was (Jesus had me miraculously meet the client to correct the error in this book) – and Jesus got this to happen exactly on the same day when I had just typed the error! How is that for Jesus helping us exactly on time! This is also clear evidence for me personally, that God is helping me to type this book now in the year 2017 (and helping me daily, even as I am actually typing each page)! WOW! Thank you Jesus for showing me you are always nearby!

The only way to thank God for such amazing things as this is to try to live our lives in the ways He has led us to understand (as pleasing to Him). And the main way that pleases Him is: for us to live our lives as His friends; trusting Him and asking Him for help to understand and to do things each day. Then, as we ask for His help to do things, the people around us will experience His-Love and His-Wisdom (working through His instructtions to us – as benefits for them and us as well).

<u>Bankrupt – Factory Solution</u>: I had one client who was financially on the edge of a cliff and just about to fall off into bankruptcy. It looked as if they would have to close their doors forever because nobody would loan them any further funds. In addition, they had recently written out more checks for total amounts which far exceeded what funds they had in the bank. A lot of checks were going to be bouncing because there wasn't enough cash in the bank to cover all the checks which were already mailed out. It was also very obvious that they were not going to be able to pay all of their employees their wages for the current week's pay, which would have to be paid within the next 7 days.

I went off to a Catholic Church at lunchtime to pray for wisdom and for help, and I was inspired by Jesus there with a need to go back to their office and to take a tour throughout the whole facility. I was inspired to look for opportunities to increase cash flow quickly.

I began my tour of the facility in the shipping area and then proceeded into the factory. I was very surprised to notice that there was a 50-foot long wall in the factory –

with shelves from the floor to the ceiling – which were all filled with Finished Goods Products (ready to be shipped out). I asked the production manager why all these products were sitting there in the factory collecting dust. The production manager very proudly explained to me that "all of these products were stocked here to protect the company's slogan of 'Always being able to ship product-reorders more quickly than our competitors could do.'"

I was inspired by Jesus to call a meeting of the partners that afternoon so I could tell the partners that they could not afford to be paying all the costs of keeping large inventories of stock right now because cash was extremely tight. And I also was inspired to convince them to have an immediate tag-sale on the very next morning. Then, early the very next morning the partners and their key people called all the major customers and offered all these extra-products at great discounts (on the condition that we were allowed to ship for immediate COD cash payments in that week). We explained to the customers that we had a temporary cash problem and we also had some products we could rush to them, at special prices because we had over-run some past orders.

The customers were blessed by God to have a loving and caring heart, and they really wanted to be helpful to us. We were able to sell about 80% of the finished goods products at an average discount of 10% in just a few days time. This produced enough cash to TOTALLY solve the cash problem and to also cover their next payroll day. I am convinced that God worked this miracle to save this company from going out of business -- because we did sincerely ask for Gods' help. Jesus gave us enough time to turn everything around, and He then helped the company to succeed from that point onward. Thank You Jesus!

An Unusual Industry, and # 777: I was inspired by Jesus in prayer, to create a new business-flyer and to send it out to business leaders in order to offer my consulting services to some new potential clients. While I was mailing them out, Jesus nudged me to send one to a company in an industry which was foreign to me. I had no prior experience in that industry at all, so I talked to Jesus about it for a while because I felt that I did not know enough about this industry and their products and services. Eventually, Jesus convinced me that I could be helpful to the organization in many other different ways like internal controls, operational improve-ments, and cost efficiencies.

Well, they did actually call me in to evaluate their operations and performance. When we did meet, their leader told me that he was a man of prayer and that God had led him to call me ... as follows:

Just one week before our actual first meeting, their leader had closed his office door, and he was praying quietly for God to help him with a lot of stressful business problems that day, and Jesus had inspired him saying: "I am sending you a business consultant to come in and evaluate things for you." Just then, at that exact moment, he heard a knock on his office door, and his secretary came in and said: "I know you are trying to solve some business problems right now and I thought you might like to know that we just got this interesting flyer from a business consultant whom you might want to meet with."

How amazing it was that God told the leader I was coming, and that God had my flyer reach him at that precise moment when he was hearing: "I am sending you a consultant."! That would have been enough of an amazing miracle for me -- but God even went further to show me that He had drawn us together for this project ... as follows:

As I opened their "One-Write Checking Account checkbook" on my first day of the assignment, I noticed that the very next check number to be used would be # 7770 and I could see all ten of the next ten blank checks sitting there on one page -- waiting to be used (that is; numbers 7770 through and including 7779 were going to be used on the very first week of my assignment). After they were used, the next number would obviously be 7780 and no longer in the 777 series of numbers. I felt Jesus smiling in my heart as this happened because the number 777 is held as the holiest number in history and it is often used to signify the permission, participation, or approval of God. The good spiritual meanings of numbers is explained in Exhibit-A of this book.

For me, seeing this series of numbers with ten 777's (on my first day there), reminded me that God had told me to send my flyer to this (unusual industry client) and that it did reach the company Leader precisely on time as the Leader was praying for help – and precisely as he was being told by God that a consultant was being sent to help him! In addition, my actually seeing that the next 10-checks were all going to be starting with the number 777 was a specifically timed miracle for me also because it was happening only on this once in a lifetime day … just as I was beginning the project. If I started the project one-week later; I would have never noticed this. The number 7,770 (starting with the number 777) will not happen again in this company until after they have written out another seventy-thousand (70,000) checks first.

I only stressed that they need 70,000 checks to be written for this number to show up again because I am absolutely impressed that God had me start with this client on the date where I would see and understand the fact, that their checkbook was all set up for me to notice this miracle at this time in history (and also 'exactly' on the first day – as I was just beginning the project)! So, it was practically a once in-a-lifetime miracle to see their checks when they had reached #7770 before their next #77770.

When you look at Exhibit-A, you will notice that Bethlehem, where Jesus was born and Golgotha, where Jesus was crucified – are both located at 777-meters above sea level. That fact should impress everyone that

777 is a very holy number indeed.

======================================

Client 555 Car Event: I met with another regular client, and we decided to meet for lunch at a local restaurant. While at lunch, we began to talk about the significance of numbers in some of the religious events in history, and I explained that the number 555 is often used to indicate the word GRACE -- which also means: "The Presence of God."

The client was excited to hear this because his mother always told him that something GOOD was happening every time she saw the number 555 as he was growing up. Then, after his mom passed away, he began to also notice that the number 555 was always showing up whenever good things were happening in his life now too. So, he was delighted to hear that 555 indicated GRACE: "The Presence of God".

Then we received the following clue-miracle that God was really with us at our meeting. For you see, when we walked out to our cars, whereas my car was on the left and his car was on the right when we entered the restaurant, there was now another car parked right between both of us, and it had a license plate number 555. God is great and amazing to give us these miracles-clues!

Unfortunately, many people miss all these co-incidence-miracles because they do not realize that God is creating all the props and circumstances in order to show His love to each one of us (daily)!

Kill the Promotion (Steal the Job): I was in line to become a Senior Manager in one of the companies I worked for. I had worked hard and earned the promotion, but another person in the company wanted the promotion instead. He actually formed a group of people to agree with him on some un-truths about me in order to get me fired (promising them that if they supported him, that they would be well-cared for by him after I was gone). He apparently reasoned that if he got me fired, he would then get the promotion instead of me.

But God had some other plans. For you see, on the day that he and his co-conspirators were launching all the forged documents and lies about me, it was the feast day of St. Anthony of Padua -- (and Jesus had nudged me to be sure to go to morning mass before I walked into the office). I therefore, thanks be to Jesus, walked into the office with the Holy Presence of Jesus from morning mass residing within me in the form of The Holy Blessed Sacrament of The Holy Eucharist, from mass.

As I walked into the building, I stopped by the office where the conspirator was having his meeting to get me fired (although I did not find out about the purpose of the meeting until the next day). I had stopped by merely to say good morning on my way by the office he was using. However, the secretary outside of that office stopped me and told me that he asked her to not be interrupted and she would leave a message for him to call me later.

I later found out from attendees in his meeting that precisely as I stopped by to say hello that he had a sort of nervous breakdown and had to be rushed to the hospital for psychological help. The people he was meeting with did get him care from some capable medical professionals who were called in; he tearfully told the people at his meeting (while he was being taken to the hospital) that he did not know why he was always trying to get Tony (me) fired and was always spreading lies about me. He admitted that I had done a lot to help him with his career – but he just kept finding himself hating me without being able to explain why. I too, was sad; I thought he was my friend!

I attribute all of my protection in this matter to Jesus Christ our Savior. It is notable that Jesus nudged me to get to morning mass beforehand and Jesus also got me to notice that it was the feast day of St. Anthony of Padua. Then, as I was walking into the office where the conspirator was meeting, I was carrying the blessed sacrament of Jesus in my body because I had just attended morning mass – and that presence of Jesus which we carry with us from Holy Mass each day is truly all-powerful as many saints have already taught us and proven to us in history.

My boss and I developed a plan to help the man recover and to also find employment elsewhere after his recovery. Fortunately, I worked for a wonderful man and a great company in an era where companies tried to do the right things for their employees in situations like these.

<u>Peaceful Surroundings for Clients</u>: Often, when I am meeting with clients who are having a lot of uncontrollable stresses about their businesses, I try to encourage them to spend some time in peaceful meditation each day, to get in touch with Our God. God does help all those who do call upon Him for help, but we do need to ask for help.

I normally recommend ways for them to do this and gladly join them for the first couple of times so I can explain how I have benefited over the years in each method I recommend.

On one occasion, I suggested that a client who was always stuck in their office, loaded with stressful issues and working long hours, should get out for a walk in a local peaceful and beautifully-landscaped cemetery, just to walk there for daily exercise and also to pray and ask Jesus for wisdom each day. Catholic Cemeteries are all blessed as holy grounds when they are opened, and they are also great holy places to walk in and pray in, both for the repose of souls present there, and also for our own needs as well.

I drove the client to a really great cemetery, which I had

used often and which radiated peace and the presence of God. There were many beautiful religious and angelic statues at that cemetery which always helped me to think about God and heaven as I walked along there. Jesus nudged me to ask the client to pick the parking place for us to use. The space we used was about a ¼ mile in diameter.

The client picked a very nice and peaceful spot to park in. Then, as we got out of the car to begin our peaceful and prayerful walk, he became excited and called me to come and look at what he was stunned and shocked by. The client had picked a place to park where -- when he opened the door to get out of the car -- he came face-to-face with a tombstone with his exact name on it. The tombstone was of a man with the exact same: first and last name, as my client's name ... but for a man who had died about 40 years earlier.

The client took this co-incidence miracle to be a definite clue from God to spend more time in prayer -- and at this cemetery from then on. He told me that he really felt that Jesus had nudged Him to pick that place to park on that day. It was a good thing that Jesus had inspired me to let the client pick the parking spot so that the client could see that this co-incidence miracle was indeed from God and specifically sent to the client directly from God. It would not have meant the same thing if I had picked the parking spot instead of the client doing it on this day.

It all was a beautiful and remarkable moment. And I was able to experience this and see the transition in a man who now radiated more and more peace every time we met after that day. Walking in a cemetery and asking God for wisdom works well for a few of my clients and surely works really well for me personally too. Somehow God seems to be more present and real in a cemetery setting.

Another place to get this peace is to visit an empty Catholic Church and to sit and speak with Jesus there as well – because the Blessed Sacramental Presence of Jesus is always there waiting for visitors. You do not need to be Catholic to visit an empty Catholic Church. Jesus blesses all those who do visit Him there, near the tabernacle, where Jesus waits for those who come to visit. You also do not need to be Catholic to visit a cemetery, either.

The wisdom we get from going to morning mass, or by going to spend time with Jesus during the day (perhaps at lunchtime) is a tremendous amount of wisdom. Jesus solved many business problems for me in my daily visits with Him for many years in that way. I highly recommend taking some time every day to get to a quiet place (at least 1-mile away from where all the daily stress takes place) and to just ask for God's wisdom about all of the problems and issues in our daily lives. God always has all the answers; we just need to spend time asking God questions and attentively listening to Him speaking in our hearts and minds (as He answers every question, one-at-a-time).

Sometimes, it is even best not to ask any questions at all – and to just ask Jesus to tell us what He wants to tell us instead. He knows all things, and He often tells me things that I have never thought to ask Him about if I just sit and wait for His words.

PRECOCIOUS, By God's Design: I heard a priest explaining that we all gain wisdom from God when we do things like read our bibles, pray the rosary, sit quietly and listen to Jesus speaking to us in our hearts and minds, or attend daily masses. He explained that all these things are methods of getting close to Jesus ... and the more we do these things, the more we come to know and sense and enjoy the holy and close presence of Jesus in our lives.

We can all attend daily mass too, even if we are only spectators at mass because perhaps we are not Catholic. Non-Catholics are welcomed at daily mass even though they should never go up to receive The Holy Eucharistic Bread, which is given to Catholics at mass. Non-Catholics need to discuss receiving The Holy Eucharist with a priest before attempting to do so because it is a holy sacrament, blessed by God Himself at each mass, and there are requirements and dispositions for our souls that are required of us before we can approach and receive this holy sacrament (God's actual Presence). St. Paul warns us in scriptures that we must never receive this Holy Sacrament unworthily:

> "1 Corinthians.11 [27] whoever, therefore, eats the bread or drinks the cup of the Lord in an unworthy manner will be guilty of profaning the body and blood of the Lord."

When I miss daily mass, I notice that I do not have the

same feelings of closeness to Jesus which I usually feel after I do attend daily mass. This is a spiritual gift from Jesus, whom we receive when we all swallow the Holy Presence of Jesus in the Blessed Sacrament each day. We cannot possibly bring ourselves any closer to Jesus than to personally appear at morning mass to receive His Holy Presence into our own human bodies. Daily mass was created by Jesus at the last supper (2,000 years ago) to give us all a share in His life. We can co-exist with Jesus, within our own human bodies, through the Eucharist (Ref. John 6:53).

In business, I often notice times when I feel led or nudged by Jesus to check on some policy or procedure or to get up and go and ask someone a question about some project. It is so amazing to me how often these nudges become miracles. It makes me look smart and precocious, but I know the wisdom all comes from Jesus ... and I try to make that clear when I get undeserved compliments.

In one case, I was put in charge of solving a huge problem: (Why had the company lost well over $500,000 worth of inventory each year, over the past three years)? After checking all of the other common causes of a problem like this with very little success, I prayed and was inspired by Jesus to check to see if the computers were calculating the values of inventory correctly. We were on an average cost system which means that the computer has to constantly re-calculate the "average cost per unit" every time new units are purchased and received into inventory.

So, Jesus nudged me to get up and walk over to our computer group who had programmed the inventory system on their own instead of purchasing a pre-canned-system to use – and we found the error was exactly that sort of error, which nobody would have expected except for being inspired by God to ask. In fact, the computer people even told me that the specs for the program did state that what I described was exactly what they had programmed the system to do. When I checked, however, it turned out that the computer programmer did not follow his supervisor's instructions. He had made an error in the programming which caused the annual $500,000 problem.

I found many instances like this in my business career – where Jesus nudged me to check things, just in the nick-of-time. After that happens to us about 3 times a day ...

we begin to notice that it has to be God giving us the ability to know things. This just makes us look PRECOCIOUS and smart, but we know the truth is that we are really being blessed with wisdom by Jesus, our best and perfect friend.

If we are doing things to get close to God each day like going to mass, reading the bible, or saying the rosary, then God sees and knows that we are trying to co-exist with Him and trying to be His friend (and I have noticed that when God sees us trying to reach Him ... that He then decides to meet us more than half-way). God has made each one of us to be His-Personal-Friend, and He does not waste any time helping us to find Him as soon as He sees us looking for Him.

The #777, Client Confirmation: ... I had to book two clients who had each called me for an appointment. I sensed Jesus nudging me to meet with my current client before setting up a meeting with the newer client for that day. I agreed to meet with the current client at his home because he also had an office in his home as well. As I drove over, I was tempted to wonder if I had misunderstood Jesus and perhaps the other client might have needed my help more quickly. I began to doubt!

As soon as I walked in the front door; I noticed their teenage daughter was working on her personal computer. Then, before I had even gotten through the doorway yet, she excitedly blurted out in a loud voice saying: "Yikes: I have 777 emails in my inbox to be read!" Since 777 is the number indicating God's Permission, Participation, or Approval – I knew that I was in the right place, precisely as I walked through the door, by hearing the teenager's #777-statement. The timing of the teenager's comment was too timely and too precisely-perfect for it not to be a miracle, especially since I had just begun to doubt which meeting I should be attending just before I arrived. In addition; Jesus also said in my heart: "See, you are in the right place."

This is another example of why I often say: "After God be-friends us; His miracles automatically become a part of our daily lives too!"

God Blessing the Seventh Day
William Blake (c. 1805)

Courtesy of Wikipedia

<u>Chapter 05</u> – Family Miracles ...

It might help readers to know that each person in my family has also experienced many miracles in their own lives as well. This book is about some of the miracles in my life and there are times when I experience a miracle at the same time that others in my family are experiencing their own miracles as well (often in the same event and in the same time zone too).

Even when we do not see miracles in our own lives on certain days, it is still wonderful to see our family members experiencing their own miracles. Miracles help us all to believe more fully in God, and they help us to grow more mature in faith. God allows us and wants us to share our miracles with others in order to give others hope as well.

Part of God's plan was to create families. The family cell is where we learn to love and to care for others and to be cared for by others. It is also the place where we learn to navigate through the dynamics of living with others who have different likes and dislikes from our own.

God obviously intended for us to exist in the form of families by the ways he created human beings to be both male and female and then telling them to go out and increase and multiply.

<u>My Son's Den Mother:</u> My son had decided that he wanted to join the Cub Scouts since a few of his friends were already Cub-Scouts. My wife, Julie, and I discussed it and decided to participate, but my wife was unable to attend the first meeting with the parents, so we agreed that I would attend for both of us and I would summarize things for her later.

When I arrived at the first parents' meeting, I was surprised to notice that all of the other parents were all moms (I was the only dad present). I quickly learned that the parents, who led the cub scouts, at least at that time in our area; were all called "Den-Moms," not "Den-Dad's." I think my face was a bright red for the whole first meeting. Many wonderful moms tried to assure me that it was fine if I wanted to be a Den-Dad because they would help me whenever necessary. One of the most knowledgeable women present even handed me a book to read which outlined the things we Den-moms (or dads) do for our sons in the program. She told me that I would see proof in this book that it is really okay to be a Den-dad.

I flew to California on business the very next day, so I brought the book with me to read on the plane. We got up above the clouds where the sky is beautiful and clear and where the clouds look like a cotton carpet beneath the plane. This is pretty high up and it makes me think of Heaven when I fly above the clouds. This was a great time for me to pull out the Cub-Scout book to take my mind off of how far above earth we were. I do not like being up that high without a parachute!

Almost immediately as I began to read the little book, I noticed that the book said: "This year, Eric's dad had decided that he would become the Den-mom because Eric's mom was too busy to commit for the year."

Yes, you guessed it; my son's name is Eric too! Can you please imagine the precision of this miracle with me for a moment so that we can both glorify God? Notably ... Someone wrote a book about Den-moms and cited that Eric's Dad was going to be a-Den-Dad for that year. And one of the moms just happened to have an extra copy of this book to give me on the previous night. And I was already feeling very close to God at this elevation above the clouds before I read the words which just now gave me goose bumps. Some people call events like this (merely a coincidence), but that is a short-sighted decision!

For sure, you can imagine how dedicated I was to be a good Den-DAD now that I knew Jesus had arranged for a book to be written in history that said (Eric's Dad was going to be the DEN-mom this year). And this was actually happening to me and my son ERIC on that day too.

Thank You Jesus for this miracle which I have treasured for many years!

==================================

<u>My Daughter's First Car Purchase</u>: My youngest daughter Tanya had decided to purchase her own first car. She asked me to go along with her since it was her first time in purchasing a car, just in case she needed some minor help. She had called ahead and already picked the exact car she wanted and all we needed to do was pick the color and the interior from the many models they already had on the lot for her final selection. Then, we would sign the paperwork and be on our way.

Unfortunately, as we began to sign papers a lot of additional costs came up for things which they should have explained to her beforehand because what we thought was part of the original price had now become extra costs. The extra costs then made the loan amount higher and then the monthly payments became too high for the intended budget.

The short story is that they were trying to take advantage of her at the final signing. Accordingly, as a father trying to protect his daughter, I naturally took the whole thing personally. They thought they could deal with her alone since she was signing the loan and I was just there as a dad. As I began to debate and try to squash each cost-add-on, they had to call in other higher-level managers to make decisions until we got to what seemed like a marathon-conference with 4 of them on their side of the conference-debate. Every time I asked a question, I would have to listen through all 4-sales-minded-people trying to convince me that they were right to add the cost to her loan. The last man they brought in was about 7 feet tall and I think around 450 pounds (we still joke about how their pinch-hitter was more like Goliath coming in for the kill).

What we were originally told would take about 30-minutes, really took about 90-minutes because each question required them to get a higher authority to approve the price. (I think this is what they call water-boarding.) I personally felt as if I had aged by 5-years or more during the process. The biggest event to make me age the most was when they each had to PROUDLY give me a detailed-scientific-lesson on why they had to undercoat the car to protect the outside bottom of the car at a price which I thought was insane. After they concluded all four of their proud lectures on undercoating, I was blessed and inspired by Jesus (who was trying to keep me calm and focused for the whole time I was there) to say the following calmly and courageously – as if I was King David with my slingshot ready to slay Goliath. And so I said: "Well, if undercoating is as crucial and vital as you all said – then it most-naturally must have been an item the factory forgot to do before shipping the car here to your lot with faulty undercoating. Therefore, since the factory messed up and left it undone, you need to charge the factory not us for the cost." So, we made it a deal breaker and we basically got them to cover the undercoating cost while we paid for some other things instead.

What I did not tell you above was that I was interiorly praying to Jesus throughout the whole ordeal, and I was trying to do what I believed Jesus wanted me to do and say in the whole episode, but I did not see any clues at all because things were happening so fast that all I could do was keep asking Jesus for help and then to say whatever came into my mind at each moment. All I had was my faith that Jesus was guiding me (even when I felt annoyed and angry and hurt about how they were trying to take advantage of my daughter to get more money for their car). I was reminded that Jesus had promised to give us the precise words to use when we are trying to be good and Christ-like in situations like this. So, I trusted that, and I kept saying what I felt Jesus wanted me to say ... even after their own Goliath came into the room.

Then at the end of this ordeal, as we walked by the new car on the way out, my greatest concern was that perhaps we had just purchased a car which Jesus did not want us to purchase. I was tempted to think that perhaps Jesus was expecting us to cancel the deal and to leave without the car, but then, I did see the following miracle-clue.

Can you glorify God with me now, please? For you see, as we were passing by the new car on the way out, the salesman asked me to read the car PIN number to him for his paperwork forms (and the PIN number ended in # 777) which is the holy number that writers have attributed to God in history over the past 2,000 years and which The Faithful-Jews have also held as a holy number in history for centuries). Jesus had me notice this 777-pin-number at the very end of this ordeal, and He consoled me for trying to be a good dad who also got a great deal out of a sales-team of (3-men and one Goliath). When God sends me a miracle-clue like this one, He also touches my soul – so I do know it is a clue from Him. As Jesus said in Holy Scriptures:

John.10 [27] ... "My sheep hear my voice, and I know them, and they follow me."

I guess by now it is becoming obvious that we need to be able to talk to God and to listen to God in order to know and do His will. The reason many people do not have many miracles in their lives is because they are not looking for the miracles to turn up in what many call coincidences. But many miracles, in fact, do look like a coincidence.

In addition, if we are not asking God what to do and not trying to do what He tells us to do, then we are not co-existing with Him and not noticing His actions in our dally activities. Exhibit-C will help anyone who wants a quick refresher on how to have conversations with God if Chapter 02 above has not already helped you enough to explain the 3-phases of having conversations with God. Exhibit-A explains the meaning of the # 777 (which confirmed we did purchase the right car)!

My Son's First Car Purchase: We had just relocated our home residence, and our children gave up a lot in friends and their favorite entertainment places and many more potential places for a better social life (in Connecticut). We had just moved to a small town in a remote area of Alabama as a result of another job-change. Our teenage son, Eric, had his heart set on a specific car, which my wife and I agreed to help him to purchase in order to get started; so, he could then make the car payments later after starting a new job.

So, we planned out a day for the car-search by lining up dealers to go to visit and to find this "ideal car." We called ahead and even had some newspaper ads showing some sales-by-owners to consider as well. Each time we could not find the perfect-car at the place we were visiting, we would naturally consider other cars there too, and talk about them before leaving for the next dealership. We spent about four hours visiting several places with absolutely no success at all, and everyone was tired. My son was notably discouraged, of course, and we had prayed beforehand and felt certain that God wanted us to do our shopping on this exact day, especially after all the careful planning we had done beforehand as well. It was a mystery as to why we were not succeeding. Jesus got me to suggest that we should stop for a while and talk things over at a small diner which I knew about, which was just down the road from the last dealership we visited. Nobody seemed to care too much where we stopped so long as we could stop and collect our thoughts and relax for a while.

Please do help me to glorify God here, will you? Because just as we drove into the diner's parking lot, we saw the exact-identical-car (and also the exact-color) which my son was sure he was going to find on that day. We had really just found the exact year, make, model, color, and price we were looking for (and there was a FOR SALE sign on it too). We just had all of our prayers answered – and it was sitting there waiting for us at the diner parking lot! We called the phone number on the sign and gave a deposit on the spot. The Holy Bible tells us to enjoy and <u>find delight</u> in living and acting daily with and close to God in our lives. The Bible Psalm 37:4 says: "<u>Take delight</u> in the LORD, and he will give you the desires of your heart."

In a way, I was so pleased that we had to take 4 hours to search and consider many other places before we reached the diner. If we had just gone to the diner and saw the car for sale immediately, then, we would not know that all the other places we checked did not have the car beforehand. So, the way things wound up happening is exactly what convinced us that this was not a mere co-incidence (and that in fact it was a clear miracle). See, we knew that no other place had the exact car we were seeking because we had already gone everywhere else!

We were Relocating for the Seventh Time: It was never fun to go through the obvious hardships of pulling up stakes and giving up friends. And there was also the giving up of past vendors and the stores that you have come to trust. Moving away from family was always very difficult too. All of our relocation moves were all job-related, so my career sure seemed to be the culprit. I often felt and noticed that moving was painful for my family, but I rarely had any choice.

Seeing what my wife Julie had to give up during each move was also painful. My wife, who has passed on now, was very artistic and creative, and each time we moved, she would design things with great passion and love -- which made it obvious that "Julie lived here." Each time we left to relocate, I could see how hard it was for her to take down all her artistic and creative decorations, which often would not fit into the décor of our new home. It saddened me to notice the hardship which moving placed on her too. She was a wonderful wife, and I am comforted now to know that she finally knows for sure from her place in heaven how much I loved her for all of our 53 years of marriage.

We owned a condo which was in a condo-complex of

400 other condos, and there were already 20-condos for sale all around us and at a far better pricing per square foot than our place was. In addition, the real estate market was not doing well, and total sales in our area for condos were getting worse every week. We had to get our intended sales price for our sale in order to pay off the two mortgages which we had on the property (2-years of unemployment necessitated a second mortgage).

We were given a miraculous opportunity to move to a place where we would be able to survive with the family-budget we currently had. We just needed to sell our condo before matters got any worse. So, we prayed like we were sinking on the Titanic, and like nothing less than a miracle would work. We prayed about our condo's selling price and dropped it as far as we could drop it. And then we buried copies of The Miraculous Medal of The Blessed Virgin Mary around the condo entrances so as to bless all who entered the condo. We asked The Blessed Virgin Mary to please help us to sell the condo in time.

A young couple from the first group of shoppers who came along miraculously agreed immediately to our price and gave us a deposit (and it was on the feast day of St. Rita of Cascia). I mention St. Rita with great joy here because our last name is Coscia – and this was an unexpected (same-sounding-name-miracle). Some people would call this just a coincidence, but I can tell you that when God gives you a miracle, something inside of you tells you that "it is truly not a coincidence." What great odds! ... Sold on the feast day of St. Cascia!

The next thing that was especially noteworthy was that the neighbor across the street from us had a license plate number 777 (which is a holy number in history attributed to God as explained in Exhibit A attached). On many mornings, as I was pulling out of my driveway, I would see this neighbor pulling out at the exact same time as me. It was un-believable how many mornings I saw this. I think the average was three mornings a week over a 10-year period. The mere thought of moving away from this 777 daily morning event after all these years seemed wrong somehow to me. But I was stunned when I learned that just before we actually moved away, that this neighbor was moving away too, and about 4-weeks before us. I have no doubt that this was another miracle because God was showing me that if I did not move at that time, then I would still not be seeing that 777 three times a week anyway because it was moving away at this time too. Once again, I had evidence that God lovingly makes things clear to us if we do talk to Him about our problems.

Wonder of wonders! After we moved and got to our new address, we noticed the container number which the town had assigned for us to use for our weekly garbage collections -- (the number stenciled on our garbage pickup-bin was 777). So now I could see the number 777 as often as I went to dump my garbage into the main bin outside of our new residence. As usual, God had a great plan all along! Seeing this garbage bin number 777 might seem like a coincidence to some people, but my heart leapt with joy when I saw it because I could sense that Jesus had replaced the car plate which I used to see at the old address (only three days a week) with this 777 stenciled on our new garbage container (for me to see daily instead).

On our first day in our new town, I went looking around for a new church to join, so I drove to several churches to visit and to see where my spirit might feel more at home. The very first church I went to visit had a white pickup truck parked right next to the door which I had entered for my visit, and its license plate had only three things on it (D D D). I asked Jesus about that and He helped me notice that D is the fourth letter of the alphabet and the D D D means 4 4 4, which is the Holy Number which signifies the Holy name of The Blessed Virgin Mary (ref. Exhibit A). Well, that was awesome because the church I had just entered was therefore perfectly named because it was named St. Mary's, and it was already dedicated to The Blessed Virgin Mary. This also reminded me that we had placed medals of The Blessed Virgin Mary around the entrances to the condo and asked for her help to make the sale so that we could move to this new town. Thank You Jesus, for sending us clues as we try to walk with you and do your will Lord!

It took me about a month to get my first business-consulting client in my new location. When I went to their place of business for my first meeting, I noticed that there were two car license plates in their parking lot (# 555 ... and ... # 777), and both parked right outside the building I was entering.

Later, as I was leaving my meeting, I asked my new client if he knew who owned those two vehicles and they said: "Yes – one belonged to the husband and one belonged to the wife." (Info: The number 555 stands for God's Grace and 777 stands for God's permission and participation). I knew God had a plan in giving me my first client with this clue – especially after the hardship of relocating so far away from my last home. We had moved about 80-miles away and I did not know any businesses in this new area. It was very soothing and comforting to sense that Almighty God had planned for me to see these two plates at my first client visit in this new area. After 40-years of seeing numerical miracle clues, you can tell when Jesus is sending a number clue as a personal miracle. And as I indicated above, Jesus impresses it on our hearts to notice – whenever He sends us a miracle.

In summary then ... We had placed medals of The Blessed Virgin at the entrances to the condo, seeking her help with the sale, then we sold to the first group of visitors who came (on the feast day of St. Rita of Cascia with our name being the same except for one letter). Then the license plate number 777 which I did see 3-days a week got replaced by our garbage bin #777 (which I will see every day now instead).

Finally, as I was looking for a church to join I found St.

Mary's with a DDD (444) clue parked outside the doorway as I left. And my first clients in the area had license plates of 555 and 777 (ref. Exhibit-A).

Baptism of Our Baby – "Saint Xander": Our daughter Lisa was pregnant and ready to give birth to her third son. He was already expected and already named Xander (a form of the name Alexander) and he was lovingly expected and prepared for with all kinds of preparations like the special room and all the new things we would need to welcome him with, like special clothing and furniture and toys. Unfortunately for us however; he was born into heaven and not onto earth – because he had already died just 1-day before the scheduled delivery and he was stillborn at the time of delivery.

This was hard to bear for everyone but most especially for my daughter who knew about the stillbirth; but only the day before delivery. Her doctor had said that everything was fine just two days earlier. Lisa had to go through the process of delivery anyway and then go through the sadness of a funeral instead of the joy of celebrating Xander's birth. There were many things to get through and to get over and another stress-causing issue was a spiritual question of: "Was Xander now in heaven even though he was not able to be baptized before he died?"

I was asked to answer this question for our family because it was a serious and sad-concern. I was not being asked for my personal opinion. I was being asked "What is the True Answer." So I did the research, but there were pros and cons and I was not sure I really understood the research data I was reading. I wanted to be sure not to mislead my family because of my own hopes and desires interfering with the truth. Fortunately; on the very next morning I attended morning mass and I was able to consult with a priest I knew and trusted about all of this.

The priest lovingly explained that the church's teaching in cases like STILLBIRTH is that we can trust in God's Mercy and Love in such cases. We can do this basically because we know God is love and all that God does is done in love; and we know that God would not lovingly prevent a stillborn child from entering into The Kingdom of Heaven. That would be contrary to everything we known and believe about our great God.

In addition, I was also told that there is a spiritual

baptism called "Baptism by Desire." This means that a person who wants to be baptized, but dies beforehand; is already baptized by desire. And the desire of the parent or guardians is also sufficient for a child to also become baptized by desire (in cases where the child dies before the Baptism could actually be performed).

Well at this point, I was relieved and blessed with facts to bring good news to my family. I could not wait to tell them that Xander was already in heaven.

On my way home I was led to stop at a local cemetery to walk along the paths and pray my rosary as is my custom when the weather is good ... and, an amazing thing happened as I began to walk. Jesus had me stop at a tombstone at the top of the hill I was walking on, and Jesus told me to brush the heavy bushes away to read the name on this very old tombstone. When I did brush away the bushes ... I saw that the name on the tombstone was Xander. Then Jesus asked me to look down the hill at the 3rd row down the hill and to go down and look at that tombstone too. That stone was lined up perfectly with the stone I was standing next to. So I walked directly ahead and perfectly in a straight line down the hill to see the stone in that row. The bushes around this very old stone were also really overgrown, and I had to work hard at reading the name on this tombstone. I got a chill up my spine when I read the name on that stone. The stone was 40-years old, and the person buried there had died 40-years earlier. But the name of the person buried there was Identical to our Xander (in both the first and last names too). This means that Jesus knew 40-years ago that I would be walking here on this fateful day; after hearing that our baby "Saint Xander" was baptized by desire and was now in heaven. And Jesus also knew that Xander was going to have the very same last name also as the person buried here 40-years-ago. I felt the closeness of Jesus at that moment (and also the closeness of Xander, whom I had never met). How amazing it is to experience these perfectly planned miracle-clues of our great God! God really plans miracles centuries ahead of us!

Please notice this miracle with me now so we can both glorify God about this wonderful gift. ... Jesus had actually nudged me and prompted me to notice both tombstones with Xander's first-name on both of them as I happened to be walking along and saying my rosary (and both tombstones were obscured by bushes which I had to brush away in order to read the names on the tombstones). Then, Jesus got me to notice that the second tombstone (which was 3-rows down the hill and exactly lined up with the stone I was standing near) – and that second stone -- had both of Xander's first and last names on it!

If I were making a movie about this miracle I would never make it sound like this, because nobody would believe it could ever happen in this way, and yet; God did make it happen -- and I experienced it too! We need to help people realize how great our God really is and how much He loves us by our explaining the meticulous and awesome steps God actually does take, (even in the tiniest of details); in order to achieve the miracle gifts He sends to us. God is present in even all the tiny minutia of our daily lives and we can notice His love in the way He does things. I mean when we really observe how intricately and amazingly God produces His Miracle-Gifts for us – we get a pretty good idea of how much He must REALLY love us.

My Wonderful Wife Julie (Passed away after 53-years): My beloved wife Julie had gotten ill on the "Holy Thursday of Easter Holy Week," which is the commemorative day for The Last Supper in the bible.

This was on April 17, 2014. After that, she was ill and in and out of surgery for 4-months. There was spine surgery, kidney surgery, liver biopsy, and lung biopsy. And there were all the doctor visits and prepping and recoveries surrounding each surgery. By the fourth month of the process, we finally heard some good news -- and that she was doing amazingly well in spite of all the cancer scares that we had faced day after day for 4-months! And she looked really healthy and looked really well now too, after 4-months of looking really worn out and weak.

So, we had great hope now based on how things looked at this point. Then, about 5-days later the doctor called and said that cancer had spread into the blood system and the best Julie could hope for was maybe 18-months longer to live (but only if she would immediately enter into the 6-month long chemo-therapy program he prescribed). He said that if she did not enter the program that she might have only 6-to-10-months to live. She took 24-hours to pray about it and she decided that she would not enter the chemo-therapy program. I was sad at what this meant, but I could see that she had her mind made up and talking about it did not help. Jesus inspired me to be quiet and be still and to support and comfort Julie in this difficult decision. We could talk more about it later on as things progressed. Jesus basically got me to realize that Julie needed time to be close to Jesus as she was adjusting to this very difficult decision. It was hard on me as a husband who wanted to protect her by nature, yet was unable to by ability. But Jesus got me to understand and to wait. Two days later, the doctor called again and said that the latest tests indicated that she had only just a few weeks to live. The 6-to-10-months we had thought she might have, just now became only a few weeks. Within just two more days' time, we were then told that Julie only had one day longer to live, and perhaps really only a few hours left. The past 5-days felt like a rollercoaster ride of steady bad and shocking news.

This 4-month-period was all very stressful and exhausting for both of us. We had many doctors to talk to and surgeries and recoveries to go in and out of, and then going into and out of the nursing homes a few times too. But now we were home with hospice nurses helping us cope with the final 24-hours. Our heads and hearts were spinning from how fast we went from expecting we had possibly 10 more months to spend together to now (suddenly) only having perhaps 24-

hours left!

Our children came to stay with us to keep watch and to comfort their mom in these final hours, and they encouraged me to go and nap for a while -- assuring me that they would call me if anything changed or if they needed me. I was grateful for the help and support so I went to catch up on some sleep.

At roughly 4:30: AM, I heard Jesus in my soul awakening me as I slept and Jesus said: "You need to go and see Julie now, it is almost 4:44 AM." I know this sounds so totally un-believable, but it did happen exactly that way. I looked at the clock and it was 4:33 AM. I got up quickly and went to be with Julie, and it was not very long afterward where she began to take her last 3-breaths of life. I was stunned because it seemed as if this was a dream. I had never seen anyone pass away before and this was extremely hard because it was my beloved-wife-Julie (my better half for the past 53 years). I began to talk to her to comfort her because I was taught that people can hear sounds and voices during these final moments of life. Julie was in a comatose state at this point. I watched in sadness to see her taking her last 3 amazingly long and slow and "very-deep-breaths."

It was so amazing to me that she seemed so relaxed and calm and totally at peace ... and I felt the close presence of Jesus and Mary there with us during Julie's final 3-last-breaths. After Julie exhaled for the third time, everything stopped, and I knew she had passed on to be with Jesus. I was sad, but I also felt a very peaceful Godly-Presence too.

I can't explain it in human terms, but I am positive that I felt the peace of heaven as I saw Julie taking her last 3-breaths in such a peaceful way. I had seen her put up with a lot over the past 4-months in surgeries and recoveries and all the poking and testing she had to endure with her normally beautiful attributes of great peace and patience. I had seen her at her very best level of patience and peace during these 4-months.

But this ending-peace was a peace which surpassed understanding! I feel certain that she knew she was going to heaven (and I sense in my soul that she saw something in those final moments which gave her the peaceful expressions which I could clearly recognize on her face). I still miss her terribly, and it has been three years now since then, but I am so happy for her to be where she is with Jesus. I keep imagining how wonderfully happy she is in heaven as I go on now without her nearby.

Exactly after Julie's last breath, Jesus asked me to look at my watch and it was exactly 4:44 AM. In history, authors have used 444 to indicate The Holy Name of The Blessed Virgin Mary. My wife had a strong devotion to The Blessed Virgin and often slept with the rosary in her hand. In addition, Julie had also gone to Medjugorje where The Blessed Virgin Mary has reportedly been appearing to villagers there ever since 1981.

My sadness for my loss at this moment seemed to be held captive by the miracle I had just experienced at 4:44 AM, and by the miraculous peace I had just noticed on Julie's face. I was sort of frozen in time at this moment. I had just been lovingly awakened by Jesus, precisely on time at 4:33 AM, in order to be by Julie's side as she was to take her last breaths, and also as, I believe, Jesus was coming with The Blessed Virgin Mary to take her into eternity at the holy moment of 4:44 AM.

Julie and I had talked often of how Jesus and Mary do come to get their faithful friends at their moments of death, so we both knew what these final moments might be like (although I had never witnessed a person dying before). In addition, Julie had always stressed to me how sad she was in her life because she had missed being with her dad (by just a few minutes) when he passed away, and she would often cry about it when telling me how empty it had made her feel in life (to have been perhaps just 3-minutes away from him as she was driving toward his hospital bed when he passed into eternity many years earlier).

Something inside of me convinced me that Jesus and Julie did not want me to feel the same sadness that Julie had felt by missing her dad's final passing, and that is probably why I heard the voice of Jesus awaken me to go to be by her side 11-minutes before she was about to enter heaven. Over the next few weeks, I was able to release my sadness a little bit each day, and as I did so, I was always comforted by the memory of being awakened by Jesus to be present with Julie at exactly 4:44 AM as she entered into eternity.

I firmly believe that Julie was taken into heaven on August 6, 2014, at 4:44 AM to be with all the saints and angels now. It is especially meaningful to me that this date in 2014 was the feast day of "The Miraculous

Transfiguration of Jesus," which commemorates the day when Jesus appeared among some of His apostles on earth while radiating light and appearing to them as if He was an angelic and holy being on mount Tabor. Somehow, I have come to understand that my beloved Julie was also transfigured on this feast day as she entered into heaven now as a new creation, and as a spiritual being.

Over the next year, I was awakened precisely and exactly at 4:44 AM (and no less than 50-times), sometimes even twice a week. This was a very great gift from Jesus to remind me so often that Julie was okay and happy with Him and The Blessed Virgin Mary as I was adjusting my life to struggle and to get along without Julie. I can't explain it now, because I do not fully understand it myself, but I feel something like a part of my being is now walking around in the Kingdom of Heaven. I feel like Julie is just on the other side of a thin veil that separates us now, which keeps me from seeing her. I feel as if one day the veil will open up and there she will be -- (immediately and precisely on the other side of this thin veil).

I hope you will glorify God with me now in all of this

and in what I am about to write here below. Because on 03-14-17, just after I had finished typing the above paragraph; I immediately took a break, and I wound up reading some of the March 2017 issue of The *Catholic Transcript magazine* from the Archdiocese of Hartford, Connecticut. I wound up reading pages 21 and 22 in that magazine entitled "A HOLY DEATH." Significantly, the article is a recap of a woman who died on October 9, 2016, and who had also been devoted to the Blessed Virgin Mary. The article spoke about how this lady said that she did see The Blessed Virgin Mary coming to take her into heaven as she was passing away ... and then it said that she (Mrs. Dube) "passed away <u>at about 4:44 AM</u>."

Jesus nudged me to read that magazine article at precisely the right moment (after Jesus had led me to first type the above page about my beloved Julie's passing at 4:44 AM before I went to take a break). Jesus also assures me that Mrs. Dube did indeed pass away <u>"at 4:44: AM."</u> Thank You Jesus for leading me to this amazing *Catholic Transcript Magazine* article as a confirmation of Julie's passing and exactly as I was typing this miracle today! This miracle surely tells me that I am supposed to be <u>typing up this book, on this</u>

date – 03-14-17!

One of the promises of the Blessed Virgin Mary is that she will be with us at the moment of our death if we are devoted to saying her daily rosary while we are alive. Julie was very devoted to saying her rosary every day, so I am very certain that The Blessed Virgin came to help her enter into eternity at 4:44 AM on that day.

Here is some amazing information about things I did notice after my beloved wife Julie had passed away:

1. The last check number in her check book -- before she would have to order more blank checks -- was number 4440.

2. The last outstanding check from her last bank reconciliation which she was waiting for to come in yet was for a check in the amount of $4.44.

3. She had two small bottles of cosmetic products from Johnson and Johnson which she used (which both have contents notes on them -- which state: "Contents: (444 ml)."

4. Her computer password was revised by her just a week before she passed away to end with # 444.

5. Three people (who were personally very close to Julie) called me within a couple of weeks of her funeral and told me that they were awakened at 4:44 AM at least once since the funeral.

6. As you already know from the above miracle story ... Julie passed into eternity at exactly 4:44 AM, and that number is the number used to indicate The Blessed Holy Name of The Blessed Virgin Mary.

7. The *Catholic Transcript* ran an article about Mrs. Dube who also passed away at 4:44 AM ... and that article did indicate that Mrs. Dube said that she experienced The Blessed Virgin Mary coming to help her enter into eternity.

8. Tradition tells us that Blessed Mary has promised to be with us at the moment of our death if we are dedicated to saying her rosary every day.

Thank You Jesus ... for all of your great kindness to Julie and me in this entire 444-miraculous-event Lord. Most especially Jesus, I sincerely thank you for waking me precisely on time to sense you welcoming Julie into heaven with your mother, The Blessed Virgin Mary.

<u>Chapter 06</u> – Church Related Miracles …

After discovering that God really did love me by the evidence of so many co-incidence-miracles which He has sent to me in my life, I began to form a habit of spending time with Jesus in prayer at His Church. I would stop by during the day and especially when I had problems to solve in life. I have found these church visits to be of great value in my life. Sure, Jesus is everywhere, of course, but we need to get away from the noise and the distractions of our daily activities, sometimes. Humans have always sought out a holy and blessed place to sit and pray alone with God throughout all of history. It can be on mountain tops, in temples, in churches, in cemeteries, and in many other places, but it always helps to know that the place was dedicated and blessed by priests through a special and holy dedication process and ceremony.

Even Catholic Cemeteries are spiritually blessed and dedicated to God and holiness when they are created and opened. The Church also keeps The Holy Blessed

Sacrament enshrined in a tabernacle inside of its churches for all to visit and to sense Christ's presence when they enter.

I hope the miracles shared in the following section do help to convince some readers that God does bless us for honoring His Church and other holy places of worship which have been prayerfully consecrated to God and to His saints here on earth.

God's Directional GPS (within us): I was working as a teammate on a Catholic Cursillo weekend retreat. There were about 20-men attending the retreat and there were another 20-men working as the retreat team. Cursillo, for those of you who do not know, is a non-denominational Christian movement which was born in Spain and which began to spread from Texas and across the USA in the 1970-1980 time-period. Cursillo (which means "a Short Lesson in Christianity") uses a weekend-retreat to explain how we can become good close friends and brothers with Jesus by spending time with Jesus and also by spending time with other like-minded men who also wish to befriend Jesus. There are also similar retreats for women where women are shown how to become close friends and sisters with Jesus as well. The following miracle is about one of the men's retreats I worked on during the 1970-80 period.

At the end of the retreat weekend, the retreat teammates use their cars to drive all of the retreatants to a wrap-up-building and to the final ceremony (usually at a Church) where The Holy Mass is celebrated and where final talks are given to send all of the men back into the world ... after they have spent a weekend getting a lot of peace, joy, and camaraderie with other men, who all have "experienced Jesus as a personal-friend."

I was new to this area of Connecticut and I did not know my way around, and this was way back in 1977 (before i-phones and GPS systems were invented). So, I asked some of the team members to be sure not to drive off too quickly out of the parking lot, and to not lose me as we all drove over to the church in our car-pool-caravan. I was told that the church we were using for the wrap up was about a 30-minute drive from where we were having the retreat. They assured me that they would keep their eyes on me in their rear-view-mirrors and stop to let me catch up if the traffic separated us on the way over.

I wound up with only one man (one retreatant) with me in my car for this car-pool-caravan, to move from the retreat house to the Church. Surprisingly, there was only one car left in the parking lot when I got there. Everyone else had taken off and this last car was leaving just as I got to my car. So I rushed to catch up to it, but it got away from me quickly because the driver was obviously late and wanted to catch up with the team. He was not one of the men who agreed to let me follow him, so he just dashed off assuming that I must be okay.

Matters got worse now, because after I pulled out of the parking lot, I realized we were in the outskirts of town and in a heavily-forested area which was far from the main roads (with no way to get directions); and the car I was chasing, had already turned left or right -- so that I did not know which way to turn after I had pulled out of the parking lot.

I pulled over and sensed Jesus telling me that He would guide me to drive to the correct place. But, I had never been here, this was a heavily forested area, and it was very lightly populated with very few houses in my pathway. Worse yet, I found out later that I also had to cross through about five (4-way-stop-intersections) ... so

I was never sure if I should turn left or right at each of the five 4-way-stop-intersections.

So Jesus inspired me to ask my co-pilot (the retreatant) to pray with me for the wisdom of which way to go at each stop sign. So, at each stop sign -- we stopped and prayed and then turned left or right or went straight, whenever we both got the same inspirations from God at each stop sign. Fortunately, the weekend did cover this process and the techniques so my co-pilot knew that it was a process we could use. Fortunately, I did not have to convince him to pray for directions.

Well, after driving for about 25-minutes and not seeing any of the team on the road, I began to doubt that I was really getting my directions from God. I began to doubt even though my co-pilot and I were getting the same inspirations about which way to turn at each intersection (I just figured that we could both, just be wrong)! The devil is very good at coming to tempt us to doubt like this at the moments when we are most-vulnerable.

At the very next 4-way stop sign; I prayed, but with deep doubts and we got a sense to turn right. So, I took a deep breath and expected complete failure because I had no idea where I was or if I had driven in the completely wrong direction for the last 25-minutes. We had spent a lot of time trusting in Jesus and going only where our consciences had felt God nudging us to go – straight, left, or right.

Wow! There it was ... right there as we turned right ... we saw all of the team's cars and all of the men rushing into the church. Jesus even left us one parking spot right next to the road and at the main entrance. My passenger said: "You know, you should move to Hollywood, you had me convinced you were lost all during that ride today."

That was really very-funny to me; my passenger really thought I was kidding. He has never believed me even though I tried to convince him every time we met. What a joy this was, and I have used this same GPS-Method often ever since then because Jesus can always direct us if we ask Him what to do and where to go – if we have a little faith and believe!

Please let us glorify God together about this miracle -- We had stopped at five (4-way-stop-intersections) over a 30-minute time span, and trusted that Jesus would help us to turn right or left ... or to go straight ahead. Jesus absolutely did guide us at each stop sign, and we arrived on time!

(Psalm 32 states: I will instruct you and teach you the way you should go; I will counsel you with my eye upon you).

God Opens Doors For Us: As a business-consultant and coach over the past 15-years, I have visited many cities and states in the USA – and I had many opportunities to visit many beautiful churches in that time.

Many times in my life, I have felt the call of Jesus to come in for a visit as I was passing by a church. On several occasions when I was asked to come inside, I would have to seek for a parking spot nearby within the city limits and walk back to the church (especially in a very busy city like New York, New Haven, or Hartford, Connecticut). But then I would get to the front door and find it locked. If I had walked a long distance, I would become perplexed at how I could be called to come in, only to find the door locked. And then sadness would come over me because I had expected to have another wonderful and inspiring visit with Jesus and now I could not even get inside. I would naturally wonder if I was only imagining Jesus calling me in, so I would begin to doubt that Jesus had ever talked to me at all in the first place. The devil is always tricky, trying to get us to doubt the truths about God and God's Loving Friendship with all of us who try to befriend God.

The first few times this happened, I would walk away saddened and hurt and doubtful. But one day, I got an inspiration to go and try all of the doors before I would walk away (and honestly it was a day where I had problems I needed to talk to Jesus about ... so I felt like I might be justified to be annoyed if I could not get inside on this special day).

There were 5 other doors to try after I found the front door locked. So I proceeded to go around, door after door, trying to get inside and when I got to the very last door I found that someone had not pulled it totally shut (because I could see the door was slightly opened and the latch near the round handle had not fallen into the hole on the door frame ... so the door was just dangling there waiting for me to carefully (very carefully) grab the door -- and not let the bolt slip into the lock. Just before I pulled it open, I sensed a Holy-Fear at thinking that perhaps Jesus or an angel was on the other side. Perhaps they had mercifully come to open the door for me (since this was the last door and I was pretty sad and running out of hope by the time I got there to open it). I also imagined that God or one of His angels had set the door up for me (just based on the way the door bolt was just dangling there -- and only a-light-breeze-away from becoming locked).

Well, I got inside and nobody was there except Jesus both spiritually and also present in the tabernacle in the form of The Holy Eucharistic Bread. I always have the most amazing talks with Jesus there in His Church, and Jesus makes me so comfortable and certain that I am indeed a friend of God. Just sitting there listening to Jesus speaking to my heart and soul obviously gives me (and anyone else) great strength and courage.

I have approached locked churches no less than 20-times now over the past 20-years – and practically every time, if I check all the doors, Jesus arranges for one to open for me. I think that in 20-times now, only twice were the doors all locked. And that was because Jesus was teaching me a lesson at the time. In about 5 of these 20 times, I had other people with me as witnesses to confirm this great loving miracle-gift from God.

In one case Jesus had me tell a friend (who came with me to visit) to check one side of the church doors while I checked the other side. When we both arrived at the back of the church, after finding all the doors locked, Jesus assured me that there was one door open on my friend's side of the building. Gently, so as not to offend, I asked my friend to please let me double check because I felt like Jesus was going to allow us to get inside. I had taken this friend here from his busy schedule to show him a precious piece of artwork inside, and it took us 40-minutes to get here.

My friend said: "Sure, go ahead, but I did really carefully check all the doors already." I could sense my friend was hurt that I sounded like I doubted him, so we checked my side again first and then went to do his side next. My friend followed me and when I got to the first door to check – it was ajar. This meant that someone (God?) had opened it up for us after my friend had already passed by earlier. My friend was now very-positive this was a miracle (and I told him that I absolutely agree) because I have seen these ajar-door-moments many times before.

The Tabernacle Breeze: On one occasion, I was in an empty church and sitting about 20-feet away from the Tabernacle (where Jesus resides in the form of The Holy Eucharistic Bread, which we call "The Blessed Sacrament"). I had been to this church almost daily for about two years at this point.

I was sitting where I normally sat each day when suddenly a cool and gentle breeze began to blow on my face and it was coming from the tabernacle, as if a fireman's fire-hose was connected to the Tabernacle, and the other end of the hose was about 5 inches in front of my face.

As soon as I noticed this cool gentle breeze on my face – it immediately stopped. And then it immediately began to blow on my face again, but this time; it was blowing up at me from the floor (from about 15-feet in front of me, and about 20-feet off to the right of me). The breeze was blowing on the right side of my face now instead of directly at the front of my face.

Without thinking at all, I just had a gift of Instant-

Knowledge from Jesus inspiring me that: "Whatever was blowing a breeze at me from the tabernacle a moment ago, was now blowing at me from the floor in front of me (and off to my right)." So I got up and walked over to the front corner of the church and saw a Holy Eucharistic Host lying there on the floor. It had obviously been stepped on over time, and it looked as though it was there for a few days after the Sunday mass had been said about four days ago. Jesus needed me to retrieve His host!

This same miracle happened again about two years later in another church which I was visiting (except the Host was in a different spot on the floor). Jesus was so wonderful to me to give me this miracle twice in my life. Both of these miracles have proven to me personally that The Holy Eucharistic Bread is indeed a living and Life-Giving-Force as both Jesus and St. Paul said it was in the Holy Bible as follows:

Matt.26 [26] Now as they were eating, Jesus took bread, and blessed, and broke it, and gave it to the disciples and said, "Take, eat; this is my body."

John.6 [53] So Jesus said to them, "Truly, truly, I say to

you, unless you eat the flesh of the Son of man and drink his blood, you <u>have no life in you</u>; [54] he who eats my flesh and drinks my blood has eternal life, and I will raise him up at the last day. [55] For my flesh is food indeed, and my blood is drink indeed. [56] He who eats my flesh and drinks my blood <u>abides in me, and I in him</u>. [57] As the living Father sent me, and I live because of the Father, so he who eats me <u>will live because of me</u>.

<u>1Cor.11</u> St. Paul said ... [23] For I received from the Lord what I also delivered to you, that the Lord Jesus on the night when he was betrayed took bread, [24] and when he had given thanks, he broke it, and said, "<u>This is my body which is for you</u>. Do this in remembrance of me." [25] In the same way also the cup, after supper, saying, "This cup is the new covenant in my blood. Do this, as often as you drink it, <u>in remembrance of me</u>." [26] For as often as you eat this bread and drink the cup, you proclaim the Lord's death until he comes. [27] Whoever, therefore, eats the bread or drinks the cup of the Lord <u>in an</u> <u>unworthy manner will be guilty of profaning the body and blood of the Lord</u>. [28] Let a man examine himself, and so eat of the bread and drink of the cup. [29] For anyone who eats and drinks <u>without</u>

discerning the body eats and drinks judgment upon himself. [30] That is why many of you are weak and ill, and some have died.

Thank you Jesus: for this holy gift of your presence in The Blessed Sacrament.

<u>**A Very Bright Car Light:**</u> Sometimes Jesus calls His friends into a Catholic Church to have a friendly visit and chat, and Jesus really does enjoy having friendly chats with all those who come to visit Him there. Over many years now, Jesus has proven to me that He loves me more than I could ever love myself ... and I know He enjoys chatting with me ... (although I personally often wonder why He enjoys talking to me -- a tiny spec in the universe). Jesus enjoys talking to every one of us!

One day, as I was rushing around and trying to complete a lot of errands, I suddenly felt a nudge to stop inside as I was driving past a Catholic Church. I felt Jesus calling me in for a chat. So, I parked my car outside the main doorway to the church and I went inside for an invited chat. As we were chatting, I closed my eyes. I usually close my eyes when I need to slowly and carefully absorb some amazing inspirations which Jesus sends me. In one of these brilliant and penetrating moments, wherein I sensed the Great Love of God toward me – I opened my eyes and noticed that the statue of "The Resurrected Christ" (which was hanging on the wall next to the tabernacle) was surrounded in a bright light coming in from the outside window. All of the rest of the wall where the life-sized-statue was hanging was NOT lit up at all (just only that statue was radiantly lit up).

After I noticed the bright light, and I felt Jesus wanting me to notice this attention-getting-moment, I looked around to see where the light was coming from. It was coming from my car outside. I noticed that I had parked in the perfect and precise spot – so that the sun was now bouncing off of my car window and into the church window. The light was coming in at the right slant and degree to come inside through two windows. Amazingly, the sun had to reflect off the car, then into the window of the foyer, and then through the next window so it could reach and reflect upon the statue at the front of the church.

Jesus Himself revealed all of the creativity and correct positioning of all these factors to me, so that I could grasp and realize the magnitude of this great miracle-gift just before Jesus then said, "And you had to be sitting here, exactly at this moment, and you had to park your car exactly where you did park it – before the sunshine came into its place in the sky just now. Can you see now why I called you here at this moment and had you park where you did park?"

I have learned a long time ago that if we do not observe and ponder these types of coincidence-miracles, we miss out on many miracles in our lives. God creates these moments for us, as gifts for us, His friends. I also noticed in the above miracle that the sun was moving across the sky at just the right speed for me to see this miracle as I was there because 5-minutes later the sun stopped reflecting inside the church. The sun had moved on and was not reaching my car outside any longer.

A Giant Sun-Tan-Miracle: On another visit to chat with Jesus in His Church one day, I felt Jesus teaching me that just sitting there facing "The Holy Blessed Sacrament," helps our souls to receive a SPIRITUAL NOURSHMENT. We receive this nourishment even if we do not even speak a word. Jesus said it is just like sitting in the sunshine at the beach, which tans our bodies. Sitting in the church near the tabernacle gains Godly-Spiritual-Radiation for our souls. It is almost as if our souls get a bit more of a sun-tan each time we visit Jesus there in His Church ... near His Blessed Sacrament.

On the next day, I went to a Catholic lecture at a retreat house ... not realizing that the whole hour's lecture was planned to be specifically all about the same Holy-Eucharistic-Bread and Tabernacle. (WOW): I was pleasantly surprised and Jesus inspired my soul to realize that He had planned for this to happen exactly the way it was happening right now. Jesus knew I would be hearing this lecture on that day right after He had taught me about the "Tabernacle-Sun-Tan" just one day earlier.

Then, on the day after the lecture, I sat down to eat my supper and watch one of the recorded TV-shows I had recorded earlier in the week. And Jesus nudged me to watch the show called "Life is Worth Living," which is the taping of Bishop Fulton J. Sheen's world famous TV-lectures from the 1950-to-1970 period. As I watched this 1966 show which Jesus had nudged me to record a few days earlier in 2017, I saw some amazing and huge evidence that Jesus wanted this item put into this book today ... because (just as I began to watch the Fulton J. Sheen show), I immediately heard Bishop Fulton J. Sheen on TV saying the following things:

"When we go to a Catholic Church and sit in the presence of The Holy Eucharistic Bread, we receive the amazing benefit of receiving the radiation of God into our souls. For just as there is a Cosmic-Radiation from the sun present at the beach for sunbathers, there is also a Godly-Radiation from the Holy-Eucharistic-Presence of Jesus – Who is present in the Holy-Tabernacle, in our Catholic Churches."

Bishop Sheen continued, "I often tell people who have spiritual questions or daily problems, to just go and sit there in a Catholic Church near the Tabernacle where the Holy-Eucharistic-Bread is kept. Sitting there and just listening to Jesus clarifies everything for us."

So you see, Bishop Fulton J. Sheen very carefully explained that we benefit from sitting in a Catholic Church ... even if we just sit there and do nothing except to let God shine His Graces upon our souls ... just like the sun-shine automatically does shine on bathers at the ocean's beaches. So just sitting there asking Jesus for help or clarification and trying to listen to ideas that come to us is really all we need to do to receive clarity and help from Jesus each day.

Likewise, both Mother Teresa of Calcutta and Saint John Paul the Great (Pope John Paul II) were both well known for spending hours visiting Jesus by sitting or kneeling before the tabernacle in a Catholic Church daily. Many of the 8,000 saints in history also spent time alone with Jesus (near His Tabernacles in His Churches). It is a great place to spend time alone with Jesus. Many saints did this every single day!

I guess now we all know that there is a SUN-Shine (Cosmic-Radiation).... and there is a SON-shine from the Holy-Eucharistic-Presence of Jesus!

My eyes automatically became tearful when I saw Fulton Sheen saying the same things (51 years earlier) which I had heard from Jesus in my soul at the church just recently. This was so amazing to me (almost the precisely same words) ... and it happened just as I was planning on how to explain all this to anyone someday.

If you would like to watch that taped 1966 TV show ...

That particular Fulton J. Sheen show was broadcast for us again at 5:30 AM Eastern Standard Time from the EWTN- TV network on Sunday 01-08-2017. You can phone EWTN-TV for viewing times at 1-866-357-4336 or check it out, on www.BishopSheen.com (or call them at 1-800-854-6316).

What a wonderful gift all of this was. Thank You Jesus!

A Confirmation of the Sun-Tan-miracle: Some of you may already know that I have been emailing out weekly letters to share inspirations and miracles which I have been blessed to notice each week. I send those weekly letters out using the address Jesus designed, With777With@aol.com. The following info was taken from a With-777-Email-letter which was mailed out after the above Bishop Fulton J. Sheen miracle had occurred. The above miracle was also sent out as letter number # 2208 by the With-777 email address on 01-11-2017. The following letter did also mention the miracle above too.

The more recent weekly Letter number # 2210 (mailed out on 01-21-2017) said the following:

"Dear Readers: You may recall that letter # 2208 about the Sunshine Miracle ... was followed by a wonderful miracle (received by viewing Bishop Fulton J. Sheen's 1966-broadcast). Well, even after I mailed letter # 2208 out ... the miracles still continued to occur as follows:

"For example, I attended morning mass on the day I e-mailed letter # 2208, and I noticed that the Responsorial Psalm-105 for that morning's holy mass fittingly said: "Make known among the nations -- and PROCLAIM ALL HIS WONDEROUS DEEDS." The bible tells us that "[w]e should be VERY excited and joyful in proclaiming what we notice about God."

"Then I noticed that the Communion Antiphon Prayer at mass, which we prayed before we went up to receive The Holy Eucharistic Bread -- stupendously confirmed letter # 2208 because it said ... "Lord, in your light; we see light." (Ref. Psalm 36). This confirmed the Sun-Tan-Letter.

"After mass was over and everyone had gone, I lingered to speak to Jesus who is always present there in The-Blessed-Sacrament in the Tabernacle. Then, as

I approached the tabernacle and genuflected on one knee in reverence, I noticed a large White-Light suddenly appear and float above the tabernacle on the wall. Its sudden arrival floating above the tabernacle stunned me and reminded me of the Sunshine-Letter # 2208 again. The floating White-Light was about the size of the 3-inch-diameter ROUND-HOST which the priest uses for holy-consecration at the altar during mass. Many people in history have seen floating lights like this in history as clues of a miracle.

"After I had gotten over being stunned and I finally gathered my thoughts, I noticed that the sunshine coming in from the side window had hit my wristwatch (just as precisely and perfectly as necessary) in order to create that White-Reflection on the wall (but only because I had genuflected exactly and precisely where I had placed my knee). If my knee had been off by just a 1/4 inch, the light-reflection would not have appeared at all. My point here is that Jesus had arranged for me to remain after mass and to genuflect exactly as I did in order for this clue-coincidence-gift to reach me.

"Then later that same day, I heard on the news that a New York detective had passed away on this very-same morning (Detective Steven McDonald). And Cardinal Dolan of New York City explained to the news media how Steve had often asked to be allowed into the church (in his wheel chair) in the middle of the night so that he could sit close to The-Blessed-Sacrament, which is present in all the church tabernacles. Steve loved to spend time there with Jesus. Steve stopped by so often that the church pastor gave him his own personal key to get in anytime. Steve was recognized as a very holy and saintly policeman who had been in a wheel chair for 30-years since being shot while on duty as a young man in New York City. It was sad to hear about Steve, but his story being aired to the world on the same day as letter # 2210 was another clue from Jesus to re-affirm letters # 2208 and # 2210 again. You can search the internet for Detective Steven McDonald's New York City Funeral, of January 21, 2017 to read about this holy and impressive policeman. He found great joy and peace in sitting in an empty church near Christ's holy tabernacle.

"Then, right after all of the above had already confirmed both With-777 letters # 2208 and letter # 2210 (about the Son-Shine at the tabernacle and the cosmic Sun-shine) ... the following thing happened ....

" ... I received an email from one WITH-777-reader who stated that <u>just seconds after reading that letter # 2208,</u> a co-worker came into their office with a huge personal and emotional problem and with great sadness. And this reader explained to the visitor the great possible positive-results of people sitting in a Catholic Church next to The-Holy-Blessed-Sacrament -- even if they are not a Catholic. This troubled person, who seemed to not be a Catholic, left the reader's office immediately to go and visit Jesus for mercy, love and comfort. Obviously, Jesus had Letter-2208 arrive at that office ... perfectly-and-precisely on time. The With-777-reader said they were amazed that the person needing to hear about the Tabernacle of Jesus had entered his office precisely just seconds after he had just read letter # 2208. Amazing indeed! "For nothing is impossible for God!"

In addition, I noticed that even before the above had occurred that I had also been in an empty church with Jesus on 01-18-17, and Jesus nudged me to reach for a book which I saw sitting in the pew next to me. Jesus said to open it up at random because He would guide my fingers to the right page. I was excited to see that I opened at random to a page where the author was explaining how he, too, (daily) visits The-Blessed-

Sacrament of a church to talk with Jesus. The book I opened at random (with Jesus leading my thumb-nails to open) was *Resisting Happiness* by Matthew Kelly ... and Jesus got my fingers to randomly open to page 32 in chapter 7.

I prepared this WITH-letter # 2210 -- to be issued today ... 01-21-17, and I noticed this morning that the reading at mass was Hebrews 9 saying that a Holy Tabernacle with Holy Bread was also used by the Jews too. You see the Jews also had holy bread in their temples each day. The morning reading at mass on this day said; in part:

"Heb.9: [1] now even the first covenant had regulations for worship and (an earthly sanctuary). [2] For a tent (a Holy Tabernacle) was prepared, the outer one, in which were the lamp stand and the table (and the bread of the Presence)."

Now, it even makes more sense than ever that Jesus has given us this holy sign to remain with us forever on earth (this Holy Bread) -- because in the Old Testament, only the Jewish priests were allowed to eat that holy bread. But now, because Jesus has come to fulfill the old laws and prophecies about Himself – Jesus tells us that

"He is the Holy Bread," which is now in our Church Tabernacles all over the globe today (for everyone to freely come to visit Jesus, whenever anyone wishes to)."

I do encourage everyone to visit an empty Catholic church whenever they can as they pass by during the day. I am confident that Jesus blesses all those who do so. You need not be Catholic to do this. Some people also just say, "Hi Jesus" as they drive by, if they can't stop inside.

God obviously can do anything He wants to do, and almost all the saints in history have spent some time alone with Jesus in an empty church during their lives whenever they had time. It is well worth the time to do so because it is most-likely the holiest place on the earth.

The Dead Battery – Mass: One Saturday evening as I was shopping at a very large Shopping Mall, I noticed an army Veteran holding up a sign at the very-busy-exit. The sign cited that he needed work or money for food and shelter. Jesus nudged me to take a few minutes and to turn my car around and to park it and walk over through the traffic to talk with the man.

We talked for a while, and he showed me a lot of evidence of who he was and explained his problems. I made a small donation and told him I would pray for him too. And I gave him copies of the Miraculous Medal of Blessed Mary. Then I went to my car, and it would not start up. I prayed thinking how this is going to mess up my Saturday night and Sunday plans because my car mechanic does not work weekends. I prayed again and turned the key again, and it started right up. But it sputtered and skipped on the way home, so I canceled my plans for Saturday night.

On Sunday morning, it was snowing pretty heavily, and I figured that I would not be able to get to the church for mass in the snow – so that solved my concerns about trying to get a ride to church. Jesus nudged me to get ready for mass anyway because He said the snow would stop and the car would start up fine. Indeed, that happened as He said.

On the way over to the church, however, the car sputtered and skipped as if the power source was going on and off a few times. I got concerned about breaking down on this long country road and maybe not being able to get to Mass -- and then perhaps being stranded after mass at our church-in-the-country, on a Sunday (with a cell phone that was out of tower-range in this area of town)! So, I asked Jesus if I should turn around and skip mass and go back home because perhaps I had misread His inspiration to go to mass today after all. But Jesus inspired my soul to hear Him say: "No, go on ahead; your car will be fine." Then, I noticed that the car I was following had a license plate that looked like a spiritual clue (although I could not see it clearly). Jesus said, "Yes it is a clue which I did send you – so do speed up a little so you can see that license plate before it pulls away at the next upcoming intersection."

I did speed up and got a good look at the car license plate before it left the intersection and went on to a different road than I had to travel. The License plate showed: "888 444" ... and I knew I was supposed to be exactly right here at that precise moment – and to be going to Sunday morning mass. The car I was following was the only car I saw on my trip to mass, and if Jesus did not say "speed up," I would have never seen this amazing license plate as Jesus had planned (to be right-in front of me and, right-now, in order to lead me to church). I have been seeing license plate clues for about 30-years now, and I know that this plate 888 444 ...

signifies a holy and blessed message. Because of my past research, I have come to understand that some religious speakers and authors do use 888 to signify the holy name of Jesus ... and 444 to signify the holy name of the Blessed Virgin Mary. (For reference ... please see The Meanings of Numbers -- reference sheet, on Exhibit-A)

Jesus was showing me (by this license plate, which was traveling in front of me) that He had called me to Sunday mass in spite of the car battery problem and the snow – and now He was showing me, by miraculously having that car arrive in front of me -- exactly as it had done, that He and The Blessed Virgin Mary were watching over me.

After mass, the car started up just fine, and the car started right up again on the next morning so that I could drive it over to the car repair shop. However, when the mechanic went outside to start the car at the repair shop to bring it in for service (the car would not start).

Jesus and Mary had indeed been watching over me to get to mass on Sunday and to the mechanic on Monday – but the car totally quit and stopped once I got to the repair shop and into the mechanics hands. Thank You Jesus!

It turned out that it was not a battery problem after all but a loose and worn out wire which was wiggling and losing power when it wiggled at the wrong moment. I guess it wiggled as I hit bumps on the road -- and if it did not wiggle back into position before I shut off the car, then the wire did not work the next time that I tried to start the car.

I believe that the car started up after the meeting with the veteran on Saturday ... and started up again to get me to mass on Sunday ... and started up again on Monday to get my car to the repair shop – all because I had done God's-Will in spending time with that veteran on Saturday night.

We naturally do not deserve all these wonderful miracle-clues. How can we deserve anything when God has already given us everything we are and all the things we have? Even a tree or a bird cannot be worthy of anything they are either. It is only and exactly only God's infinite-love that allows us to be recipients of God's continual love! Nobody is, nor can anyone ever become, worthy of God's love.

Sometimes, when I feel very unworthy of being God's Friend, Jesus smiles in my heart and explains to me that nobody and nothing can ever possibly be worthy of God. So being sure you are not worthy is a good sign. Anyone who thinks they are worthy of God's Love is sadly mistaken. God's love is an unconditional love; we can't earn that love. All we can do is control our behavior so that we do not offend God!

Divine Mercy Sunday -- Vacation, 04-03-2005:

My beloved wife, Julie, and I went to a Christian Seminar in New Hampshire in April, 2005. We felt badly because we had hoped to be back at home in time to participate in "The Divine Mercy Services" at our parish church, but we were not going to make it in time for the afternoon of 04-03-2005. However, as we were driving home, we passed by a very nice little country church and decided to stop in for a brief visit.

After we walked inside, we learned that at 3 PM on that very day that this little church was going to be celebrating Divine Mercy Sunday (right there in New Hampshire). So we decided to linger there in town and attend their 3 PM Service. We took this co-incidence as a miracle from God who was showing us that we could attend the services here on vacation, which we were missing by not being at home on this day. This co-incidence-miracle turned out to be the most wonderful part of our vacation trip -- as you will see below.

When we did arrive later at 3 PM we found out that "Pope John Paul II" ... (canonized as a saint on April 27, 2014) ... had just passed away into his heavenly reward on the prior night -- on Saturday 04-02-2005.

Then we found out that Ivan (the visionary from Medjugorje) was also visiting this church on this same day and that he was going to give a lecture and also receive an inspired message from The Blessed Virgin Mary as well (after the 3 PM service, before we left for home that day).

When Ivan told everyone about the vision he had from The Blessed Virgin Mary on this Sunday, he added that he saw Pope John Paul II entering into heaven and that he heard The Blessed Virgin say that "Pope John Paul II was with her today in paradise."

It was especially meaningful to Julie and I that we were

able to witness this event together because we did not know about Ivan's plans to be there at that time ... and my wife did get to meet Ivan when she went to Medjugorje to visit (where The Blessed Virgin has been appearing to Ivan and three other visionaries monthly now; since 1981).

Adding to our amazement was the fact that Pope John Paul II had just passed away on the prior evening, and it was mainly through his efforts that Divine Mercy Sunday was established in 2001 to appear in the church's formal annual calendar from then on. It is now formally a part of our Catholic calendar and to be celebrated each year (on the Sunday immediately following Easter Sunday each year). And here we were in New Hampshire, celebrating it as Pope John Paul II (the founder of this holiday) was seen entering into his heavenly reward at the start of this exact Divine Mercy Sunday date of 04-03-2005.

The Powers and Graces from God on this holy day were evident in the vision and heavenly messages which Ivan had gotten from The Blessed Virgin on that afternoon. And we also witnessed a person who seemed to be healed of some physical health problems precisely during Ivan's vision of The Blessed Virgin Mary on that day.

How wonderful for Jesus to get us to notice that this 3 PM Service was going to be held so that we could linger there and participate in this wonderful holy-day-experience! It was a wonderful opportunity to be forgiven of the entire temporal punishment still due to us (as Jesus has promised through both: St. Faustina and St. Pope John Paul II ... to all who do attend and participate in this Divine Mercy Sunday each year).

Anyone attending this Mercy-Service each year is forgiven all temporal punishments; as promised by Jesus to St. Faustina in the 1930's.

Chapter 07 – Jesus' Love and Protection Miracles ...

We can see many things happening during the "co-incidence-miracles" which God does send us each day. We may notice some things like ...

- God showing us that He is near us during our stressful times.

- God teaching us, through the new experiences He sends us.

- God guiding us, step by step (but only one clear step at a time).

- God confirming things, by making them happen as we expected.

- God loving us, and protecting us -- and just in the nick of time.

The more we notice God acting in our lives, the more we come to know His personality. We become aware of how He acts with and within us over time, and we come to a point where we know what to expect in some of the things which He does in our own particular and unique life.

I think this is because we are all perfectly created by Him to be what we are. For example, if we are a violinist, we naturally relate to God differently than a drummer or a pianist.

God is the perfect friend, and He teaches us over time how to enjoy and how to co-exist within His amazing "Divine-Personal-Friendship."

<u>God's Automatic Alarm Clock</u>: A few years ago, I found myself waking up on morning and finding that I was having conversations with Jesus as I did wake up from my sleep. It was as if I was dreaming with Jesus and talking to Jesus about things – and then simultaneously waking up while I was also in the midst of speaking with Jesus.

An amazing moment happened on another day, after my beloved wife Julie had passed on into her heavenly reward. I was still missing her pretty badly at the time, and I woke up as I was saying: "Thank You Jesus, it was really wonderful to spend that time with Julie, Lord."

I do not often recall any of my dreams, but this dream was about Julie and me riding our bikes around some country roads in places like Ireland and Jamaica and having picnics at some beautiful scenic places where the temperature was perfect for these activities. In addition, Julie and I were about 21-years old in this dream. And, after being married for 53 years it was wonderful to be back at age 21 in a dream. It is especially really wonderful at my age!

After I awoke and savored this miracle-dream for about 10-minutes, my alarm clock went off as scheduled. Thereafter, on many mornings since then, I have continued to wake up about 10-minutes before my alarm goes off so I can lay there and talk to Jesus about things before I roll out of bed to begin my day. I know this is a gift from Jesus because I asked Him to do this for me, and I do see this happening more often now. It lets me have a time to chat with Jesus before I get out of bed.

In addition, if you read what St. Paul says in 2-Corinthians 13:1, you will see that the Jews in history always looked for three-signs or clues (to be sure of their evidence). Accordingly, after Jesus had awakened me ten minutes before my alarm went off by well over 3-times, I became sure that this was a gift from Jesus. God can be very convincing indeed.

A Birthday Job: I had accepted a great position as a vice-president in a very successful company. But after I joined them, we discovered some manufacturing errors in products which were already shipped out. The products were manufactured before I had joined the company, and now they had to be recalled and re-manufactured at no charge.

The products in question were those which had made our company successful financially because the pricing was especially profitable for these products. But now, however, because we had to re-work and re-ship them, we were running at a loss on these contracts, and we had thousands of items to be re-worked.

The company just barely stayed in business during this disaster. Since I was part of senior management, I had agreed to take salary cuts in order to help the company survive throughout the period and to keep the factory workers at full-pay so that they were not penalized by this managerial error. This was a very good and conscionable company with leaders who protected workers and sincerely cared about their employees.

Things got worse because we could not work on other new customer orders during this time, so we started losing some new customers and company morale began to slip. Some of us in management had our salaries reduced by 50% by now in order to keep things afloat. Then I was inspired to utilize a spiritual-fleece (like General Gideon did in the book of Judges) to see if I should move on to another job. General Gideon's Fleecing methods are covered in Exhibit-B at the end of this book.

My FLEECE was to send out some resumes, but to keep working at this troubled company. I figured if someone called me with a job offer, then this would be a clue that Jesus wanted me to leave this company. It was not long then before things began to get tough financially for me personally at this point too.

I did get some calls for job interviews; then, one day, I decided to attend mass one evening during the Christmas season before going home ... and since it was my birthday, I asked Jesus (as a birthday gift) to get me back on payroll at full salary or to get me another job, PLEASE.

Nothing visibly happened and the next day was Christmas Eve. Then, at about 4 PM on Christmas Eve, Jesus nudged me to call one of the companies who had interviewed me so I could ask what the status of their decision was. I doubted I would get any intelligent answers because it was a holiday, but I was inspired to trust Jesus, and Jesus also got me to understand that there would be no harm in calling for status of the job because if nobody was at the office on a holiday, then who would know I called? Caller ID had not been invented yet.

So I called, and the person who had to make the final decision about hiring actually did pick up the phone and was actually there picking up some paperwork that day before leaving for the holiday. I was astonished when he said, "Tony, I am so glad you called because I was supposed to call you yesterday, but I got tied up at the airport and I just got in to town today, only just a little while ago. I was going to call you after the holiday weekend to tell you we would like you to start immediately if you can do so."

Some of what is amazing in all this to me is that I had asked Jesus for a Birthday-Gift-Job on my birthday (the day before the holiday) ... and when I called (on a holiday) I was told that the decision to hire me was made on that exact day when I had asked (which was my birthday). If I did not follow the nudge of Jesus to call on the holiday date, I would never have known that I did get my Birthday-Gift-Job (exactly on my birthday). Notably, Jesus got me to call at the exact moment when the person in charge was about to leave the office after coming in to pick up some things. Jesus' timing is always so perfect!

We need to follow the nudges Jesus inspires inside of us. And, sometimes, we need to sit down quietly someplace and talk to Jesus when things don't seem to make much sense – because for God nothing is impossible.

This was an excellent example of experiencing a co-incidence miracle. Miracles do often look like a co-incidence. But in my case here, I had asked for a gift on my birthday (and I did get it exactly on my birthday)!

You may know that we all do become more holy and

more Godly with every single prayer and conversation we have with God. I do not know how else to explain that except that the more time we spend with God, the more we become more and more like Him (our Creator and Father).

Talking to God about everything, gives us some familiarity about what it feels like and what it sounds like when God is responding to us. His voice and His thoughts always sound like our own voice and our own thoughts because He speaks to us -- through us. The more we talk to God, the more confident we are when we hear his familiar-response. God can make sure that His responses reach us (we just need to listen with our hearts and minds). When we ask God to help us He really does; He actually loved us before we were even born!

Exhibits B and C explain how to have conversations with God daily and how to discern God's Will in difficult situations.

John.14: Jesus said ... [26] But the Counselor, the Holy Spirit, whom the Father will send in my name, <u>he will teach you all things</u>, and bring to your remembrance all that I have said to you.

Matthew.7: Jesus said ... [9] Or what man of you, if his son asks him for bread, will give him a stone? [10] Or if he asks for a fish, will give him a serpent? [11] If you then, who are evil, know how to give good gifts to your children, how much more will your Father who is in heaven give good things to those who ask him!

John.10: ... [27] My sheep <u>hear my voice</u>, and I know them, and they follow me;

Please let me stress an important point here:

Just so that readers do not wonder how it is that I can call this a miracle in a company which was going bankrupt ... let me explain that, after it was all said and done, Jesus had sent me to every new and different job in my life with a specific miraculous plan (which I did not realize until I had begun to write this book).

For example ... before getting this New Birthday Job (a miracle); I had been <u>blessed by Jesus to install several improvements in the company I was about to leave</u> (and all of these things ultimately saved this company from bankruptcy). Accordingly, only with hindsight, Jesus showed me that He had sent me to this company just before it got into financial troubles with massive customer returns so that I would be there to become inspired there by Jesus to solve their nightmare. Then I could move on to the next company and job.

My point is ... Jesus had a plan for me over the past 50 years that only unfolded into my actual realization and appreciation as time moved on. We do not realize the miracles Jesus is going to work with us and through us (until they happen). But Jesus knows all about them, even before we are born.

So please do realize along with me now that Jesus did not send me to this troubled company to make me suffer. Instead, Jesus sent me there to be there when the disaster occurred so that Jesus and I working together could solve the problem together. Jesus brought all of the wisdom and power -- and I just showed up to do what Jesus told me to do. I always know that it is Jesus who really does all the good works (I just show up and try to do what Jesus tells me to do).

... Two major and important things were necessary to save this company, as follows:

(1) -- We had to rework and reship 100-thousand defective-products, but we only had one quality-control-machine to verify and prove that we had fixed the problem. Every single piece of product had to be run through this (one and only machine) to prove that it was perfect before we could ship it back to the customer.

This machine had a cost (new) of about $800,000, so we could not afford to buy another machine, yet we were unable to accept new customer orders until and unless we got the whole 100-thousand items refurbished and re-shipped first.

After mass one morning on the way to the office, Jesus told me to create 3-shifts for that quality control machine even though the rest of the employees were working only one-single-shift. This solved the problem because it was as if we suddenly had just purchased two more machines, by just adding two more shifts to each day.

The rest of the 130-employees could produce just enough units in one day to utilize 3-shifts of this quality control machine's availability. This one change alone enabled us to ship three times the quantities each day now than we were shipping previously.

(2) Then again on another day after morning mass Jesus inspired me to go in and install an assembly line – even though this would benefit some other products which we were manufacturing, which were very "Labor-Intensive." This enabled us to triple the output of that area of the factory as well -- and even on some very profitable products. We needed this extra inflow of cash pretty badly by then.

In total, Jesus had inspired at least 5-miracles in that company (to save them from bankruptcy) before Jesus and I moved on to the next company to help the next company, which was also going bankrupt.

1. We had reduced executive salaries at the start of the problem.
2. We began 3-shifts for the 1-key-machine to handle demand.
3. We installed an assembly line (like Henry Ford did once too).

4. We re-negotiated loans to pay less per month for a while.

5. We caught a thief who was sending payroll checks to their family members who were never seen at the facility but who got weekly payroll checks. The employee thief had been left in total charge of all the payroll functions. We had been paying 3 of her relatives for 2-years and nobody ever realized it until Jesus and I did a payroll audit one week and came up with 3-non-existent employees!

Obviously, the wisdom for all 5 miracles came from Jesus ... <u>all I contributed was my body</u> ... and my doing what Jesus inspired me to do each day. Jesus is always the source of wisdom, and the source for all the right answers! The Joy I experienced in helping companies in my lifetime because Jesus allowed me to do so was a great gift to me!

<u>A Job -- In the Nick-Of-Time</u>: My employer's company was sold and absorbed by a larger corporation, so I found myself out of work. I had good credentials and a lot of good solid experience, but I could not land a job. I was out of work for about 18-months. I kept getting a lot of "almost-jobs" and some part-time work but never enough to pay all the bills. I could not understand why God was letting this all happen to me, and I began to feel a little like Mr. Job in the bible. He lost every single thing he had. I figured that if I was feeling a little bit like Mr. Job, then naturally I was going to keep losing more and more (and it got pretty scary sometimes).

Telling my wife and 3-kids and my friends what was happening so often, and retelling this story over and over as they asked me how things were going, became exhausting and embarrassing too. It feels exhausting because you have to keep telling people the same sad story as each person asks you "how are you doing?" It also feels embarrassing because after 12-months you feel like a reject and a failure (unless your faith and trust in God is really very strong)!

I kept going to morning mass every day and praying and doing all the things you have to do to find work, but I was getting more and more like Mr. Job (in the bible) each day. My savings were being depleted, and I started to over use my credit cards! I started to feel like God had given up on me (but something in my soul kept saying God loved me ... just like Mr. Job also felt God's love all during his disaster).

Then things really got very bad. I got to a place where I only had 3-weeks more cash left to survive on and I was about to start begging more people for help. It was a very hard, mysterious, and scary time. I learned you can still have faith, even when you are being frightened and tempted to give up, just like Mr. Job in the bible had also experienced. Mr. Job is a great model who never gave up trusting God!

Well, I was home alone at this stressfully-exhausting point. The kids were out, and my wife was working – and I became overcome with sadness and defeatism (18 months of not getting hired will do that to most of us). I purposely, in a feeling of total failure, fell down on my butt in a corner of the room -- and I began to cry. And I pleaded with God to please do something "please!"

After about 15-minutes of deep heart-felt pleading, the phone rang and I was offered a job! It was Monday. I went in for the final interview and began working the next Monday. Two weeks later, after the cash I had left was gone, I got my first new paycheck from this new company. It miraculously arrived in time to keep our family afloat (again)!

The company told me that they were INITALLY not ever going to call me for an interview -- except that the following things had occurred:

They had gotten many other resumes to consider and my resume was pulled out as "not to be considered" because I was way over qualified for the job opening).

After they had met with all their candidates, they were still not satisfied with anyone in the pile, so they began to re-consider my resume.

Simultaneous to the above facts, their Vice-President was at a block party (picnic) on the prior weekend, and his next door neighbor (who was a good friend of mine) told him about me and the fact that I could not find a job now for about 18-months. My friend had a copy of my resume so he gave it to the Vice President right after the picnic was over -- on that exact day.

Then on the day I got the call ... on Monday ... here is what happened: (A)... The hiring manager re-selected my resume from the pile of resumes which were classified as over qualified because he did not find anyone else suitable yet. (B)... Then he took it to his boss (the vice president and the neighbor of my picnic-friend) and told him that he wanted to interview me even though I was overqualified -- to see if we can work out a deal. (C)... The vice president pulled out his copy or my resume from the neighborhood-picnic ... and they both called me on Monday to invite me in for an interview (I had been sitting on the floor crying and begging God for help ... as explained above). (D)... They were afraid to hire me because they said I might not be able to cope with being demoted 2-levels from where I used to be and to eat humble pie. (E)... I convinced them to give me a chance and I was honest about my cash problem and my 18-month search. (F)... I worked there for 10 years and rose up through the ranks by a lot of hard work, and by learning how to chew on humble pie.

Jesus inspired me to do many things at this company to help them with a lot of systems and procedures and profitability problems over the 10-year period. I also learned a lot of things which I did not know before (which all helped me to start my own Business Coaching and Consulting company after this company was sold and absorbed by a larger international company).

Incidentally, the boss who was instrumental in re-considering my resume after I had been classified as over-qualified was a very bright and kind man. A great clue was that his phone extension was # 555 ... and # 555 signifies GRACE – which means (the presence of God). Every single step above was orchestrated by God. I did not always see it back then, but now (23-years later) it is clear that God loved me way back then, and He has never ever stopped. God is always by our side and is always very-ready to help anyone who sincerely calls on Him for help.

The Optometrist Miracle: My doctor prescribed a new prescription for my new eyeglasses, and I prayed about where to get the prescription filled. Jesus led me to three places to get an estimate for the cost. I thought Jesus could have just told me to go to one place, but Jesus wanted me to go and get three estimates. The first place had a doctor who did the eye exam and also supplies the glasses, charging $400 just for the glasses; the second place charged $297, the third place was $200. All these prices were just for purchasing the glasses, the eye exam would cost extra. Jesus nudged me to order the glasses for $200.

After I got the glasses, they told me that my eyes might take a few days to adjust to the new view, but to give it a few days. Well, after 2-weeks of patience, I was positive that my older glasses were better than these.

I called the doctor who prescribed the glasses and he said; "as I told you earlier, you probably will need cataract surgery soon." After another week of blurry vision and constant tilting of my head to see better with the new glasses, I pleaded with Jesus to help me resolve this annoying problem; the new glasses were worse than the older ones I had before.

So, one morning after attending morning mass, I had about an hour's time to stay at the church and talk to Jesus about several things which were happening in my life at the time. After about 15-minutes, Jesus inspired me to get up and go to the doctor and ask him to re-check his prescription because it was worse than the prior set of glasses I had previously, and it sure did not make sense that my new glasses were worse than the old ones! I talked to Jesus about how this felt uncomfortable because the doctor had told me to expect cataracts and maybe it was the cataracts that were the problem -- and not the prescription.

Jesus patiently put up with my comments and then told me to trust Him and to go to the doctor right now and ask him to recheck the prescription. I hated the thought of walking right into the doctor's office without an appointment, and I knew the doctor was going to be annoyed because he told me to expect cataract surgery as the solution (and I was sure that I did not want to have cataract surgery right now). So I left the church to go to the doctor as Jesus had nudged me to do, but I was not happy about the prospects of what was about to happen.

I got to the first 4-way-stop-intersection and I wound up taking a right hand turn and found myself following a car plate which had a plate number 777 (the number signifying God's participation, or approval). (Refer to Exhibit-A for the meaning of numbers). I followed that car for quite a while thinking how God must be saying that I am going to the right place and at the right time because the car was going my way.

Well ... I wound up following that car through the main traffic in town and for about 2-miles (and wonder of wonder!) – it went to the same exact doctor and parked in the same doctor's office parking lot that I also was going to). Jesus smiled in my heart and said, "Yes, I did send you here from the church after mass ... and ... I did send that car to lead you exactly to the same doctor. Yes I did time that – on time for you." Wow! How amazing God's timing is to send a car to lead me there!

At the doctor's office, after putting up with their telling me that it was cataracts, Jesus nudged me to sternly convince them to check the prescription again. Finally, they did check, and surprisingly -- they agreed that they messed up and had given me a bad prescription to fill.

The moral of this story is: Leave the church when Jesus says to leave (for His timing!) ... and do what He tells you to do in all situations. Thank You Jesus for loving me and protecting me with your love!

The Amazing 77,777-Mile-Moment: Hopefully, I have convinced you by now that God will often use numbers to get our attention. Many historians, theologians, and writers have been using numbers to communicate to mankind for thousands of years. Even the bible itself uses three famous numbers in the book of Revelation as follows: (Revelation 13:18: explains #666) and (Revelation 7:4 and 14:1 and 14:3 -- explains

#144,000) and (Revelation 1:4 through 1:20 -- explains the 7-star-angels, 7-lampstands, 7-churches). If you Google the word "SEVEN" used in the holy bible, you will be impressed with how often the number 7 shows up in meaningful ways in history.

After 30-years of seeing the number 777 at the precise times when I was looking for a clue that God was nudging or loving me, I became very sure that God uses that number to signify His approval or participation.

Exhibit-A explains the good and holy significance of numbers and if you read 2-Corinthians 13:1, you can see why the Jews historically looked for three-confirmations before making important decisions:

2-Corinthians.13: [1]. this is the **third time** I am coming to you.

Any charge must be sustained by the evidence of two **or three witnesses**.

One day as I was driving to meet the president of one of my clients and wondering if Jesus wanted me to be handling this account, I noticed that the miles on my odometer on my car dashboard showed 77,770 miles traveled. I was very excited when Jesus nudged me to realize that Jesus was helping me to notice the odometer as I was headed for exit #7 where I had to exit the highway. I was excited because I was wondering if God was going to bless the meeting I was driving toward, and I was seeing a lot of sevens coming together at this moment.

Well, after I got 6-miles closer to the exit #7, I began to realize that it was becoming extremely likely now that my odometer was going to reach 77,777 miles just as I was driving off the exit ramp at exit #7, which is very exciting when you have been doing this for 30-years (because this was an amazing first for me). Jesus often assures me that He is with me when He shows me 777 during a project, and I was about to get 777 + 777 if I reached exit #7 in perfect timing (77,777 + exit 7).

Just as I was about to exit on exit #7, I saw all the miles on my odometer show up as 77,777 miles. I thought to Jesus: "Gee Lord; we should have a drum-roll or maybe some thunder and lightning go off to commemorate this amazing line-up." And Jesus said to me: "Look out of your left window and see the car passing you." WOW! The car passing me, as I was pulling off the highway at exit #7, with my odometer showing 77,777 (had a license plate number 777). WOW! I sure felt loved and protected at that precise moment. I think this is what people mean when they say "all the planets and stars were lined up!" Thank You Jesus!

If you do not see numbers to confirm Godly things in your life, that is okay too. God will send you some other things to use which will keep popping up to confirm His love with other clues. (Exhibit-A explains the good and holy meanings of numbers for your info).

Once again let me point out that we use three numbers when using numbers as possible clues from God because the Jews and many holy saints do look for 3-clues, 3-witnesses, 3-signs (to feel confident of any trends or inspirations they are receiving). Exhibit-B cites examples of getting clues as confirmations (i.e., fleecing steps).

A Dizzy Miracle of Loving-Protection: I had developed a dizziness problem and I had to walk close to the walls, and then use a cane when walking in wide open spaces where there were no walls to guide me. Sometimes, while walking up a staircase I would stumble and have to grab the railing quickly to avoid tumbling down the stairs. The whole process was very disheartening because I felt insecure to move around – thinking that at any moment, I might get worse and not have anyone present to help me. I had seen the doctors and they were treating me for a form of Vertigo (an inner ear infection). But it was not getting any better, and sometimes it would seem to be getting worse than the prior day, or even worse than the prior hour.

So, one day after 2 weeks of treatment, I got a nudge from Jesus to call the doctor and ask for some other treatments because it was just going on too long. After driving from work to the doctor for 60-minutes and finding that my doctor got called away, I was assigned to a Nurse-Practitioner who was part of his staff. Her diagnosis after consulting with some other doctors was that I should drive to an X-ray facility to get some hi-tech X-rays of my ears and head to see what the X-rays might reveal.

After the X-ray technician saw the X-rays he spoke to some doctors and came to me and said: "I spoke to your doctors and also to our doctors on staff here and they want you to get to the emergency room of the hospital near your house as quickly as you can. They have already been called and they want you to get there quickly so that they can run some other tests to be sure that you are okay. You need to get there before they close down that department for the day and weekend." This happened on a Friday afternoon and that department was apparently closed on the weekend.

I drove for 30-minutes at the highest legal speeds I could to get there quickly for the tests. After being in the emergency room for about an hour and answering questions and filling out forms (and repeatedly telling them that I was told to get here before the proper department closed), the doctor in charge of the emergency room told me that she was sending me home because she did not see any problem. I argued with her because of the 2-weeks I had spent with a problem, which she was now calling "just my imagination" – so she got extremely rude and told me that she had the authority, and they were overloaded, and they could not do anything for me at this time.

Fortunately, my wife had driven over to be with me and was standing at my bedside at that moment and Jesus had her and the angry rude-doctor standing there -- as I suddenly blacked-out -- and immediately came back to consciousness again in front of them. I personally did not notice my black-out but they both asked me if I knew what had just happened. They both saw me black-out and come back to consciousness quickly a couple of times while I personally did not notice it at all. I did not notice it because I was having seizures which only lasted a quick second or two.

I finally and eventually figured out the cause of this entire problem much later. It turned out that I had hit my head about a month earlier while working and rushing around my garage late one night. But the symptoms did not start until a few days later – so I did not associate that accident with the dizziness at all. I did not realize that I developed a leaking of fluids into my skull. This was gradually causing pressure inside my skull by reducing the normal skull-space for my brain. The squeezing of the brain by the lack of space is what was causing the quick 1 or 2 second blackouts which my wife and the doctor just witnessed. I personally did not notice the seizure at all because it happened so quickly – fortunately my wife was there as a witness.

Now, I knew why I was stumbling while walking or

running up the staircase at the office each day (it was because I was blacking-out in the middle of climbing the stairs as my foot was reaching for the next stair). The blacking-out for just two seconds was causing my foot to miss the step and stumble so that I never knew I was falling during the black-out. I only realized I was falling as I came out of the 2-second black-outs.

I have learned that this is a common problem for sportspeople like hockey or football sportspeople who have their heads knocked around. The treatment for this problem of fluids on the brain is to drill two tiny holes in the skull and drain out the fluids and then everything becomes fine --if the blood vessels have healed and have stopped leaking fluids.

All this is usually caused by banging your head on a hard object like the garage door, which I had forgotten to fully open up before rushing through it, as I was rushing to finish up a project in the garage late one night.

I listed all the steps above so I can highlight how wonderful Jesus was to me in all this. So we can notice all of the "co-incidence-miracles" here:

First, Jesus kept me from falling down stairs many

times at the office (as I blacked out and came to, on the stairs each day).

<u>Next</u>, He nudged me to insist that the doctor see me after two weeks of improper treatment for an inner ear infection.

<u>Next</u>, Jesus kept me from blacking out as I was driving for my X-rays ... and then ... as I was driving to the emergency room at 65 miles per hour.

<u>Next</u>, Jesus also had my regular doctor called out from the office so I could get to see the Nurse-Practitioner who insisted that I get to the X-ray specialists immediately, even though some doctors were telling her to just have me come back another time.

<u>Then</u>, thankfully, Jesus had my wife present when I blacked out on the stretcher in front of the angry emergency room doctor, who wanted me to go home so she could use my stretcher for the next patient in the emergency room.

<u>Very importantly now</u> ... just in case some readers might wonder why Jesus had allowed me to suffer so much

with this Dizziness-Problem ... I need to own up to the fact that God was really loving me (and not really causing me to suffer). Because the liquids which were leaking into my skull, and which were caused by me banging my head on the garage door turned out to be a total blessing from God.

For you see, I had developed an alcoholic drinking problem, and I had too much to drink on that night when I rushed in and out of the garage as I was working on a project in the garage. I had too much wine to drink and I was therefore not pleasing Jesus at all at that moment.

Jesus did a good and loving thing by letting me bang my head into the garage door and to develop fluid leakage into my skull afterward. For you see, once I finally realized (in the hospital bed now) that all my dizziness problems were caused by my drinking of wine in excess, I then realized that Jesus was trying to get through to me, and He was trying to get me to stop drinking before things got any worse.

Jesus surely got me stop my excessive drinking. I was lying in a hospital bed recuperating and reflecting on how I had actually finally stopped drinking for 3-days now. I was unable to stop drinking at home over the past 2-years, but now in just 3-days at the hospital, my 2-year addiction was gone. Jesus helped me by drilling 2-holes into my skull (because that is what it took to straighten me out).

I had tried to stop drinking for 2-years on my own, but I never made it through even one full night without drinking. I had been praying for Jesus to come and help me to stop the drinking after dinner which became an awful addiction over the course of a 2-year period. Eventually, after 2 years, I had a really bad habitual drinking addiction!

People with a drinking problem know that it starts off with what looks like very innocent, sociable drinking. Then, we start having two glasses of wine for dinner instead of one. Then in a month or so, we are up to 3-glasses with dinner, and after a year ... we are probably up to starting with 1 glass of wine as we get home from work each day (and then refilling that glass all night long until bedtime – or until we bang our head on a garage door and get two holes drilled into our skull to drain the fluids)!

I felt responsible to type the above addition to the story about <u>A Dizzy Miracle of Loving-Protection</u>, because other-wise someone might think that my best friend (Jesus) was not being very nice to me by sending me such a problem.

In the final analysis, however, Jesus was being very good to me by getting me to stop drinking any alcohol at all after He showed me that the whole dizziness story was my own fault. Furthermore, I kept asking Him to stop my drinking problem every day (for 2 years), but I was not following His daily helpful advice which was always the same advice: "Just do not have the first glass of wine at all at dinner time." Eventually Jesus answered my daily prayer to help me stop drinking -- and He did it in a very dramatic way (because I left Jesus no other choice).

If I had followed His advice for 2-years "To never even start drinking each evening – and to never even take the first drink," I could have avoided all the drama in the emergency room.

Actually, if I ever wanted to get to Heaven without having to spend probably a thousand years in purgatory for a drinking habit, I needed to stop drinking now in this life before I got to the Golden Gates of Heaven where they would most likely not let me in.

Based on the following passage in the bible, Jesus did me a great favor by letting me bang my head into the garage door. The following scripture indicates that we are going to need to overcome drinking habits (here on earth) if we ever want to get into heaven. The following scripture also indicates that there are many other bad habits we will need to stop here on earth before we die – if we hope to enter into heave after we die.

<u>1 Corinthians, Chapter 6:</u> [9] Do you not know that the unrighteous will not inherit the kingdom of God? Do not be deceived; neither the immoral, nor idolaters, nor adulterers, nor sexual perverts, [10] nor thieves, nor the greedy, nor drunkards, nor revilers, nor robbers will inherit the kingdom of God. [11] And such were some of you. But you were washed, you were sanctified, you were justified in the name of the Lord Jesus Christ and in the Spirit of our God.

By the way, Jesus never stopped being my best friend all during this 2-year addiction. I could tell He was unhappy with my addiction, but I also simultaneously felt His love too. I guess it was like we feel when we do something wrong and we look at our mother and know that she loves us ... but that she is hurt and saddened by our being less that she knows we can be. Thank you Jesus for curing my stupid drinking addiction problem!

Chapter 08– Miracles While Introducing Jesus to Others …

It is a great joy to know Jesus and to then work at introducing Jesus to others. The reason for this great joy is that Jesus helps us to do this work, and whenever we are working with Jesus by our side, we can't help but notice His miracles. Everything Jesus does is a miracle!

I am really very positive that I am not the very best friend of Jesus, but I am getting a bit better each day. The more we walk and talk with Jesus, the more we come to realize more and more of His greatness and His true love toward each one of us.

Every single prayer makes us better and more like God. The more we pray, and talk to God, (and listen to God) – the holier we become.

For me, being convinced that life is absolutely greater and happier with Jesus as our friend than it can ever be without Jesus is what compels me to help others to know Jesus. And Jesus has inspired me that He has that passion also (to help others to experience life at its best – and its best is only obtained when souls become friends of God).

Jesus himself nudges us toward those He wants us to reach out to because He knows who needs to find more of Him for happiness.

Mailing "With-777-With" Letters: I had already attended several Catholic weekend retreats by 1975, and Jesus helped me to experience His real and personal friendship in my daily life. I then became sensitive to try to help others to also experience that same amazing friendship with Jesus too. As indicated earlier, once we find great joy in a life lived with Jesus beside us all day long, we truly want to share this knowledge with those we care about in our lives. This especially is the case when we find people in life struggling with problems and who need to know the reality of Jesus being available (as a true friend to each one of us) anytime we call on Him for help.

One of the things Jesus led me to do was to publish a monthly letter (called: "With777With letters") which listed some understandings which Jesus had taught me while I was reading spiritual books, reading the bible, attending daily mass, and from having daily chats with Him within my heart and mind each day. I am told that the Dominican order of priests was originally formed with this same charism and goal ... because they were inspired by Jesus; that they were to learn about the things of God ... in order to share what God taught them each day with other very busy people, who did not have time to study and learn and contemplate what God was showing them.

I began sending the "With-777-Letters" out long before computer-E-mailing was possible or invented yet, and I did have a full-time job and career as well. I found myself typing up Postal-Cards to mail out as bulk-mail through the Post Office. These mailings had to be given to a printer and they had to be grouped by Zip-code and delivered to the Post Office banded up by Zip-code. The postage and printing steps as well as the time to type and patch the typing (because I did not type too well back then) became a big investment of time. And it took a lot of time to take a seeding-inspiration or understanding which I had gotten from God, or His Bible, or from other books which Jesus had led me to read and to try to put it into a brief postal card. So, it began to become a part-time job in many ways. Another time-consuming aspect of this job was the fact that I had to get the message onto a 3-inch by 5-inch postal card (which often necessitated finding the exact wording so that the inspiration could be delivered within the space allowed). This can take a long time, and it often felt as if I was trying to deliver a story on a document the size of a postage stamp.

As I began to send these postal-card-letters out in 1975, I would often see miracle co-incidences pop up which were clues from God to show me that I was going in the right direction. In fact, as I began to reach out to others to help people in my circle of life to also come to know Jesus, I would see signs and clues often directing me on how to do this. I hope the following examples help to show how closely Jesus works with us to draw others to Him in order to become His personal-friends.

<u>Naming the Letters (as "W.I.T.H.")</u>: One morning while I was still in the early weeks of creating and typing the first postal cards to be mailed out, I was awakened and heard Jesus in my heart and mind telling me to title the letters ("With Letters"). So before I even got out of bed, I asked Jesus why I was calling them (With Letters). I had no idea what With-letters meant. Jesus immediately responded in my heart and said: "WITH is an acronym meaning: (With, In, Through, Him) and the word (Him), stands for (Me as Jesus)." I talked more about this with Jesus before I got out of bed, and He impressed me with the fact that He wanted me to do this (I got very excited, because God had actually awakened me and actually given me directions about what to do next).

I had my doubts that perhaps I was making all this up in my mind, so I kept talking to Jesus as I dressed for work and drove over to morning mass on the way to work. Then at morning mass after the bread and wine were TRANSUBSTANTIATED and changed into the real presence of Jesus ... the priest elevated the changed and Transubstantiated Blessed Sacrament and said: "Through Him, With Him, and In Him ...." And I thought and said: "But Jesus that acronym comes out to TWIN, not WITH." Jesus responded: "Yes, and that is why I want you to use WITH -- so that it does not interfere with or detract from what is happening during the Holy Sacrifice of the Mass."

WITH-777-Letters (about 5 years later): I had spent a lot of funds and time sending out WITH-Letters in 5-years. In addition, some of the people I loved and respected (who I thought I was being helpful to) bluntly told me to STOP sending them any further letters. I got to feel rejected and thought that perhaps Jesus was telling me to stop now because we had perhaps achieved His goals. Jesus assured me that He wanted me to continue because He was inspiring the items that I was sending, and He wanted it done for reasons that would become clear to me some day later on. Accordingly, I told Jesus that it is getting costly for me and cash was tight for me at that time. Jesus responded that I would find some money in my mailbox on that day when I got home, and it would convince me that He will cover the cost of the letters so that I could stop worrying about the cost. He actually also told me how much money I would find in the mailbox. I could not resist rushing to the mailbox as soon as I got home, to see what was about to happen. WOW! A recipient of the WITH-letters wrote me a wonderful letter explaining that the letters were very helpful to them in evangelizing their circle of life for several years now and they said that Jesus had nudged them to send me the enclosed check to cover some costs. It was exactly the amount of money which Jesus said I would find in the mailbox that day. Nobody had ever sent any contributions up to that time. Jesus had just shown me that He wanted me to continue to send out the WITH-letters. Thank You Jesus!

WITH-777-Letters (about 15-years after beginning): The list which began at about 40-people had grown to about 1,000-people by now, and I had recently gotten about 10-rejections from some people on the list who said they did not get anything out of the letters I send to them and that I should stop sending them. I felt hurt because I had been sending what I truly believed Jesus was telling me to write and send out each month. In addition, I had often seen clues from Jesus confirming the messages which I was typing and sending out. These frequent and unexpected confirmations from Jesus sure did impress and stun me often because of the realization that Jesus was bothering to prove to me (a spec-of-dust in the universe) that He was sending me these messages to be mailed out each month.

Anyway, because of the rejection letters, I began to think that perhaps it was time to end this mission. I imagined that Jesus was going to give me another mission after I stopped sending out these WITH letters anyway, so why not just stop? The letters basically told of the meanings of some bible passages and also told of some miracles which I had seen in my life and in the lives others. These were all helpful things to strengthen the faith of some people, and, in addition, to energize and activate the embryonic seeds of faith of some other people.

Then on a day in 1990 while I was visiting a business client in Queens, New York (about 60-miles away from my home), I was driving by a Catholic Church. Suddenly, Jesus nudged me to park the car and come inside to talk about the "With-777-Letters." I went inside the church and prayed for a while and kept getting inspired with the idea to continue to send out the With-Letters because they really do help many people. I was reminded that the Dominican Charism and goal was similar (to help others to know Jesus as a personal-friend).

Since it was time for me to leave for my client-meeting, I got up to leave, but I was still not convinced and I also felt conflicted because I felt I was wasting my time and that I was obviously also annoying some readers who did not want the free letters at all (even for free)!

This was all very frustrating because the inspiration I was getting from Jesus in this church did not agree with my own mind's opinions. As I got to the door to exit the church, Jesus nudged me to take home a copy of their parish bulletin which was stacked in a pile at the exit-table in the foyer. As soon as I picked it up, I noticed the parish pastor's name printed on the top of the front page. The pastor's name was Father WITH. Yes, his name was WITH! Then Jesus said as I was walking toward the exit (a bit stunned and dazed): "See, I want you to continue to send out the WITH-Letters."

The above may not impact you at all because I may not have written it clearly so let me highlight that: I had never been into this particular church in Queens, New York, and I was just passing by as I was driving toward my business client, and I was praying about whether or not I should stop sending out the monthly With-Letters because I had gotten a bunch of rejection letters from some recipients. The odds of seeing this pastor-with <u>a last name of 'WITH,"</u> and located at this particular church, which was located 60-miles from my home are surely astronomically-slim. And seeing it exactly in the hour that I was thinking all of this is also a miracle. Some people might call all of this a co-incidence, but then if they do, they really should call it a co-incidence-miracle ... in order to fittingly honor and glorify God!

I have been sending these With-Letters out now for about 40-years and each time I ask Jesus if I should STOP, I am led to continue them. I get just enough feedback from readers to convince me that the WITH-Letters are helpful and that they are from Jesus and not from me. I often hear or read something the very next day, after I send out a "WITH-777-LETTER," which confirms and agrees with what the With-Letter message was. So for me, it is a miraculous experience. I am sure that I write the poor letters, and Jesus writes the great ones.

Even while writing this book, Jesus has sent me joy by sending many affirming and confirming signs that He is writing this book with me. **(Exhibit-E shows some confirmations which occurred as I was typing this book).**

Gave Cops Miraculous-Medals: You probably already know a lot about the history of the Miraculous

Medal. So let me just briefly highlight some basic things about it so you can look into it further on the Internet if you wish.

It is a medal which the Blessed Virgin Mary designed herself back in 1830. The Blessed Virgin appeared over a period of time in the 1830's to a nun who is now canonized as a saint with the name of St. Catherine Laboure'. The Blessed Virgin promised to bless anyone who wore or carried these medals on their own person. Ever since 1830, there have been countless stories of miracles which have followed those who carry and promote these medals. St. Catherine Laboure' is enshrined in a Catholic Church in France and she is in a glass see-through-casket where you can see that she is still as lovely as she was when she died. She is distinguished as an incorruptible-saint which means her body has not decayed as normal human bodies do.

Knowing that The Blessed Virgin Mary does gain heavenly blessings for all those who do carry her medals, we do people a great service when we give them copies to wear or carry with them. Mary told St. Catherine Laboure in 1830 that people should wear the medals around their neck. Then, sometime after 1981 when The Blessed Virgin Mary began to reportedly appear in Medjugorje (in what was previously called Yugoslavia), she indicated that people should wear (or carry) the medals with them in order to gain the blessing.

I assume that just carrying the medals was now sufficient in order to reduce and avoid persecutions because it is more important that each of us knows we are carrying Her medals with us than it is to always show others we are doing so. Just giving the medals to others, in and of itself, naturally tells others that we are also personally carrying these miraculous medals on our person or in our pockets.

I have been nudged by Jesus many times now over the past twenty years to give these medals as free gifts to many people and quite often to police-men and to police-women because of the personal dangers and risks of their jobs as cops.

On one particular day, Jesus nudged me to walk over to a parked police car and offer some medals to the cop sitting inside, who was on an apparent stake-out assignment. The instant I got to the car with my hand outstretched and palm opened to reveal about 25-medals in my hand, the police-woman inside the car, suddenly and surprisingly became very excited and cheerful.

She told me that she had two young boys (twins) at age 5. She explained that one day recently, she had taken her sons to a Catholic Church for a visit in an empty church just to give them the sense of reverence for the church and for the presence of Jesus residing there. She said that as they were walking down the aisle, one of the boys noticed a medal exactly like the ones I had in my hand, and he picked it up and put it into his pocket and kept it as his own. His brother felt left out and began to complain, and this mother-police-woman had to convince them to take daily turns sharing the medal because she was not able to find another one like the one they had found. She said it was becoming a huge frustration and she was at her wits end to figure out what to do about it because it should be causing peace and joy and not arguments with the kids. She was so grateful that I had stopped by with these free medals.

It turned out as we talked that her son found the medal in the church where I had been attending morning mass each day ... and he found it near the pew that I usually use when I go to morning mass. So for me, this was a double-miracle because I realized that I must have dropped the medal from my pocket (by God's divine plan) so that all this could happen the way it did for that wonderful family, and for me too! I gave her enough medals for her whole family so that now they can all have their own miraculous-medal. Jesus assured my heart that He had orchestrated all of this to unfold as it did. I had no idea that the police-woman was actually trying to find a medal exactly like the ones which Jesus nudged me to walk over to her stake-out-site and offer to her.

Jesus often nudges me to give these medals to groups of policemen and policewoman when I see them together (even if I only see two of them together) so that I can tell them all, or both, that The Blessed Virgin Mary will obtain heavenly blessings as she promised, for all those who carry these medals. This has the wonderful benefit of both cops being able to tell each other about the miracles they do encounter in their lives after they begin to carry these medals. It is more splendid when two of them can share their miracles together because I have given them both a medal at the same time. I also do this with construction crews I see on the roads when Jesus leads me to do so ... so that the whole entire crew can share their daily miracle stories with each other in the days and weeks following, after they have begun to carry their medals each day.

Sometimes, people do stop and tell me about the miracles they have experienced after carrying these miraculous-medals with them each day. The medals are all blessed by a priest before they are shipped to me each month.

More information on how to order these medals is shown on Exhibit-D at the end of this book. They are not expensive but of great value in spiritual terms. Saint "Mother Teresa of Calcutta" is quoted as having personally handed out about 4,000 of these medals in her own lifetime.

Bringing Joy to Nursing Home Residents and Staff: I have a good Christian friend who visits Nursing Homes regularly to hold meetings in cafeterias and to play some popular and golden-oldie musical CD's. He also reads some scriptures and offers some spiritual insights on topics which the residents and the staff then discuss openly afterwards.

One day, my friend asked me to come along and to give a lecture on the value and use of numbers in helping us all to notice God's Clues and God's Co-incidences. When it was my turn to speak, I explained the good spiritual meanings of numbers and I explained how we might see numbers confirming when we are actually experiencing a miracle.

Some of the resident-patients and the staff began to ask a lot of interesting questions, and I could see they understood how numbers can be good signals and clues for some miracles. (Exhibit-A explains the good meanings of numbers for your info).

One particular staff-nurse became excited and got everyone else excited when she heard that the number 222 indicated the following:

> "Being sent out 2-by-2 just like Jesus sent out His disciples to minister in the world 2,000 years ago." This number 222 -- can also indicate that Jesus is with us (Him and us, together, 2-by-2). Jesus co-exists within us, and uses each one of us (2-by-2 with Him) to reach out to more souls for

Jesus."

The nurse then proceeded to tell everyone about her vacation in Barbados and how she rented a car there, and when she picked it up (it had her most favorite number in her life as its license plate number). She sees this number 222 many times during a typical week and she said that she often sees good things happen after she sees this number during her average day. She got many people interested and excited and laughing about some of her stories about how 222 does show up in her life as a clue.

I walked out of the building feeling that Jesus and I had just helped the nurse to see the closeness of Jesus in her life. She had always noticed good things happening when she saw #222, but she did not realize God was involved until now. I felt that we had also convinced her to look at these 222's from now on as clues from Jesus to brighten up her day.

It was a great gift for me that, just as I was walking out of the building, I saw a taxi cab parked outside the main entrance waiting for someone to come out and enter the cab. The phone number on the cab to call for service was

222-2222 and it was parked exactly at the main entrance as I exited the building. For me, this was another clear signal from Jesus that He and I were inside the building together today (2-by-2) reaching out to everyone ... including "the # 222-nurse."

The Gas-Pump Evangelization: Jesus often leads me to evangelize people (to gain new friends for Him) at the gas station pumps. If we listen to Jesus in our hearts, He leads us to see who to speak to or not.

One day, when I really did not need to purchase any gasoline, Jesus nudged me to go into a gas station to get some gas anyway. When I pulled in, I noticed that there was one pump still available and that the car parked in the next bay – and next to my open spot -- had a license plate which showed only three letters: (D-D-D).

The letter D is the fourth letter of the alphabet. We sometimes get a coded clue in letters, and this one would translate to 4-4-4, which is used to indicate the Holy Name of The Blessed Virgin Mary.

My usual opening statement in these cases is to say: "Hello, I am fascinated by your license plate. Did you order it special or did you just get it by chance at the

Motor Vehicle Department?" Then, after they respond, I tell them what the number means in Christian numbers, and I hand them medals of Blessed Mary telling them about the medals and The Blessed Virgin Mary's promise. Her promise is "to obtain God's blessings for all those who do carry Her-Miraculous-Medals with them."

When I got to the end of my normal opening statement on this day, the man got very excited and said he had to call his wife right now about this because she had become very fond of the number 444 in her life and that she had ordered the DDD-license-plate to remind her of her daughter (by initials in her name) after her daughter had passed away. He was positive she would be delighted to hear about DDD meaning 444 because his wife was having a sad period just now with life in general and this might really help to cheer her up.

Well it sure did perk her up and she was so excited to hear that she was getting some medals of The Blessed Virgin Mary for her family and friends because she too generally says Mary's Rosary each day also.

I feel humbled when I notice that these miraculous

encounters seem to be definitely pre-arranged by God. For example, in the above case I did not *need* gasoline because I still had over a half of a tank left yet. But Jesus did get me to go for gasoline in that precise hour and moment when a man with a sad wife was there with a car having a license plate DDD (#444). This sure seems pre-arranged to me. It is almost as if God is a director of a movie and He arranges (as director) to have all the props in place first before He sends us into the scene to speak a special script which He places into our minds as we enter the scene.

This is the kind of joy we give to others as we introduce them to Jesus (as their co-existing friend). It's interesting that the bible has a book called "The ACTS of the Apostles" – like the <u>ACTS of a Broadway play!</u> I thank Jesus for sending me for gasoline on that day, and on time!

<u>Store Shopping (Team number 444) (with an 888 buddy):</u> I have been shopping at the same grocery store now for well over 4-years. I have often been nudged to place Mary's Miraculous Medals on some cars parked near me each time I shop. I understand that Jesus takes care of inspiring the owners of the cars later on. My role is to place the medals on the cars to which Jesus leads me each time I park my car there for shopping. The medals are neatly pre-packed inside of an info-folder with information on the history of the medals so that people can understand why I left them a medal when they open it. It clearly looks like a gift from God when they open it up because it is free and professionally described by the vendor -- inside of the envelope.

One day while I was inside shopping, I overheard a supervisor apparently scolding one of his employees by yelling out (444). He yelled this out rapidly and 3 times in a row; saying: "444 – 444 -- 444." So I politely asked the supervisor what this all meant because 444 was a holy number to me. I explained to him why I was asking and he responded that he calls out the number 444 whenever his team makes a very serious error. He said that his team knows that they made a serious error whenever he does this. I explained that number 444 is also the holy number which reminds us about the Blessed Virgin Mary, and then I gave him, and also each member of his whole team, a Miraculous Medal of their own. I told them that the medals were all blessed to be holy sacramentals by a priest already so that all they needed to do to receive God's Blessings is to carry Mary's miraculous-medals with them all day long.

Over the past 12-months already now, whenever I am shopping there and I see one of his teammates, I call out to them by saying: ("444, 444") – and they respond saying "444." It's now a reminder of Mary!

After the above 12-month period, a great thing happened. First, as usual, I had placed a medal-packet on a few cars outside in the parking lot as I was parking my car. Then, because one car had a license plate number 888; I left them a note along with the medals explaining that their license plate # 888 is a reminder in history that 888 signifies The Holy Name of Jesus. I told them in my note that Jesus had obviously blessed them by giving them such a wonderful plate. Next, when I came in to shop about a week later, the "444-supervisor" came over to me and told me that the owner of the 888-car came into the store and told him that he was very grateful for the medals which he had received on his car and he wondered if the supervisor knew who left this great note on his car. He said: "I have an idea it is our 444-customer."

The address to use to order the Miraculous Medals for your family and friends is listed in the (Exhibit-D) at the end of this book. They only cost about 15-cents each. There is also a very interesting book by a Catholic priest entitled _77 Stories of the Miraculous Medal_ (see more book info on that book in Exhibit-D).

The Poker Game Story: We were celebrating a holiday at home with some family and friends. During that afternoon, some of us decided to play cards for a while, and we were playing a game of Poker for toothpicks (not for money). We often play cards for toothpicks so that nobody ever loses any money.

While some of us were playing cards, some others began to gather around the table and watch. As they were watching they somehow got into arguing about if there really was a God or not.

This arguing was disturbing me because I have taught Sunday school now for over 40-years, and to have my family and friends sounding un-sure that there is a God means that somehow I have failed someplace. So, I asked Jesus (within my mind) to help me with what to do and what to say. It saddened me to hear them debating about God and not coming up with any good answers to end the discussion with a good and positive result. I also felt that Jesus wanted me to say something, but I had no idea what to say.

Well, Jesus told me (in my conscience and heart and mind where He speaks to all of us) to also deal the empty seat next to me -- a hand of cards – and to let the crowd watch and see what happens. My immediate reaction was that I was imagining this. I could not believe that Jesus wanted to play Poker with us, even if He was sending an angel to sit there in that empty seat on my right hand side. However, in the speed of the blink-of-an-eye, Jesus convinced me that it will be fine because I can tell everyone that: "We are going to deal a hand to this empty chair and let Jesus do whatever He wants. Maybe He will do nothing or maybe He will do something ... but all I know, folks, is that Jesus wants me to do this and to watch what happens next."

After calming them down because some of them said that we might get struck by lightning if we did do this, I finally began to deal the cards with the deck of cards sitting in the center of the top of the table, just so that everyone could see that I was not dealing off the bottom of the deck at all. We were playing 7-card-stud, which means that the first two cards and the last card, are all facing-down, while the other 4 cards are all placed facing-up as they are being dealt out to each player. The three cards shown face-down are called "the stud" which only the individual player can see. Everyone else only sees the 4-face-up cards.

I dealt the first two face-down-cards and then I dealt out the first face-up-card. I noticed that Jesus (the empty chair) got a number 7-card for His first face-up card. I dealt the second faced-up-card and Jesus got another number 7-card. I got excited now because we already had two number 7-cards for Jesus (the empty chair) and I already knew that for about 3,000 years now or more, religious leaders have claimed that the number 777 is the holiest of numbers and it is supposed to mean God's approval or participation or permission. In fact, the Jerusalem annotated bible has a footnote in chapter 7 of the book of Wisdom which explains that Jews have held the number 777 to be a holy and sacred number for many generations.

Perhaps the most convincing point I can make about 777 being ordained and used by God is this: Bethlehem, where Jesus was born ... and ... Golgotha "skull-hill," where Jesus was crucified; are both at 777-meters above sea-level. This means that God created the whole universe and when He made Earth, He decided to make both the birth-place and the death-place of Jesus to be at 777-meters above sea-level. That is pretty convincing evidence that God agrees that 777 is a very special number. The historical meaningfulness of numbers used in Christian Writings can be found in the Exhibit section of this book's table of contents (in Exhibit-A).

Well, we had to wait until the end of the hand to see what Jesus (the empty chair) had in His 3-face-down cards. What awe hit us all when we looked at all of His cards and saw that He had gotten four sevens (7777). Jesus inspired me to tell the group that Jesus got four instead of just three (777) because He could do so and because He wanted to help us to be sure and to BELIEVE IN HIM. I often tell this story when I meet people who deny or doubt there is a God -- and I also stress the Earth being at 777 meters above sea level in those two amazing places!

Producing a Weekend Retreat (Revised Key Chain): I was part of a team which was producing a retreat for a Connecticut Retreat House. I had given a copy of my lecture to a teammate to use so he could decide if we needed to make adjustments in our talks to keep our concepts in harmony. We wanted our concepts and wording to be similar so as not to confuse the audience.

After I had sent my talk to my teammate, Jesus inspired me to change a sentence in my talk to make my talk easier to understand. Then Jesus said to telephone my teammate to tell him about the change. I called my teammate and said: "Jesus had me change the last sentence in the talk to say: "She had left her keys on the kitchen table."

My teammate said he could not believe what just happened because, just before my call came in for him to pick up, he was reading a new book which he had received that day, and which he had been reading when the phone rang. He very excitedly and joyfully said: "Tony, the line I just read before the phone rang says: 'Her keys were on the kitchen table.'"

WOW! Yes there is a God and yes we can often find God in the things we call coincidences because with God, there really are not any co-incidences (even though they look that way). Essentially, every act of God is a miracle!

Nudged To Drop Off A Retreat-Flyer at the supermarket: Jesus nudged me to drive over to a large local supermarket to hand a copy of my newest retreat-flyer (and a registration form) to a manager who I knew at that store. It was a very busy time of the day, and I had no personal confidence that the manager would be available or even working on that particular day because they work on a rotational basis and their hours can be very flexible. I was totally trusting Jesus' nudge.

So, in faith, I drove over through the day's heavy traffic period, I parked my car, and then I walked toward the front door to enter in. Then, just as I got to the front door to enter, and exactly at the door frame, the manager was exiting (precisely at the same time), and she was leaving after ending her shift for that day. I got there in perfect timing (precisely perfect timing) with me going in, as she was coming outside! I was able to hand her the flyer before she would have left for the day. If I had been 20 seconds later, she would have been gone for the day and that would have made this trip of faith a failure! Yes, God's Miracles often might look like co-incidences, but they are not co-incidences when God is sending them to us!

I had driven through heavy city traffic during rush hour, and in spite of that (or due to that), I was perfectly on time! It is always a clear signal that God is involved when the timing is impeccably perfect.

Golgotha, courtesy of Pinterest (Matthew 27:33)

Called "Skull Hill" Due to the 2 Large Eyes + Nose in the Rock Formation

Chapter 09 – Summary and Conclusion

I have spent 50-years being blessed by God with many daily Co-incidence-Miracles. I have also met many people like me who have also received theses same kinds of loving gifts from God as well.

Only after 50-years did Jesus impress upon me the importance of writing this book to help others to also notice His loving presence and availability all day, and every day.

I spent a year to pull all this together and to try to deliver a book which I hope is helpful to many souls. As explained in the book in several places, I noticed Jesus breaking in on me often as I was typing this book with many clues that He was right there with me typing this book as a co-existing team. He is the wisdom; I am just the typist. As these clues kept arriving in the midst of my typing, I became so very blessed in being assured that Jesus was really creating a lot of this book with me. The parts that do not bear fruit are my parts, but the parts that do bear fruits are most assuredly God's parts.

If this book is a success, you will be looking for and also noticing at least 3-coincidence miracles a day in your own life – every day. I would suggest that you keep a piece of paper and pencil handy so you can jot down one or two words each time you see a miracle in your life ... so that at the end of a week's time, you too, will be impressed with how unconditionally God loves every one of us. Thereafter, you will be trying to convince others of this wonderful part of life – wherein we actually co-exist with, and in daily conversation with, God within us.

The more we come to know God and spend time thinking and talking to Him (as face to face friends, having two-way-discussions together), the more we will notice miracles in our lives. This is because wherever God is present and active – miracles just automatically happen.

God wants us to enjoy our life with Him. He made each one of us because He wants each one of us to be His Friend. When He made us, He placed a bit of divinity in each one of us so that whenever we want to, we really have the divine ability to become a friend of God. Without God giving us the ability and talent, how could we ever relate to and radiate some value toward our perfect and infinite God?

John.1 [12] But to all who received Jesus, who believed in his name, he gave power to become children of God.

I pray that you will consider giving copies of this book to others in your life, as a birthday or Christmas gift, so that they too can find their own miracles every day as well. Rest assured of my daily prayers for each one of you. Please also do pray for me as well.

Email me to be added to our FREE weekly email letters, about miracles and meditations. Tony Coscia -- (email to: With777With@aol.com).

Post-script:

WELL ... another Co-incidence-Miracle just happened:

The publisher and I were all finished with the book now and we had agreed with the final editing and additions of the book ... so we were finally done and excited to see how Jesus was going to bless this book and the people who do read it.

After 50 years of experiencing thousands of wonderful miracles, and after 12-months of pulling about 100 of them together into an organized book, I felt like I had gotten to the top of Mount Everest. No, actually I felt as if I had already climbed Mount Everest and had gotten back down to sea level again, because the mission was completed.

Then feeling accomplished, I began talking to Jesus about that journey and thanking Him for allowing me to be a part of all of this.

Suddenly, Jesus nudged me to take two famous books which I have, and to sit down and open them both at random -- because He wanted to give me a message.

I opened the book called *THE IMITATION OF CHRIST* written in 1391, and 100 years before Christopher Columbus discovered America. I wound up opening it at random to the section marked in the book as <u>BOOK III (chapter one)</u> -- and I read these words:

"Blessed is that man who hears Jesus speaking in his soul, and who takes from His mouth some word of comfort. Blessed are those ears which hear the secret whisperings of Jesus."

Next, Jesus nudged and inspired me to take the book called "HE AND I" (volume 1). I opened it at random and wound up seeing the last two paragraphs of the entry which was made in that book as dated January 3, 1948. Here is what Jesus said to Gabrielle Bossis in those two paragraphs (and what Jesus was now also saying to me – after writing this book with and for Him):

"You see, what pains MY love is indifference, apathy, stagnation. When it comes to ME, many people act as if I was still dead. But MY child, I am alive and I am near them, in them, waiting for them to talk to ME. I am waiting for their hearts to beat a little for ME.

I require so little, am so readily pleased. I only ask to be invited and I look after the banquet."

Well, as you probably noticed already by now, the mission and purpose of this book was precisely to have people do exactly what Jesus just told me in the above two paragraphs. This then is the last of many co-incidence-miracles which we have received while writing this book (see Exhibit-E for others).

Jesus is a wonderful God-Friend to each of us. He lovingly just now showed me these random words in two books to tell me that He was pleased with this book and that this book will achieve His purpose.

I pray that God will bless all of you who do try to listen to the voice of Jesus speaking in your own soul.

Amen.

Total Eclipse of the Sun during the time of this book's production - August 21, 2017

Courtesy of Wikimedia

Exhibit-A: Meaning of Numbers -and- Address:

1) Mailing Address:

Tony Coscia

P.O. Box 301

Willimantic, CT 06226

Email: With777With@aol.com

2) Meaning of "Good Numbers in History":

Christian Historical Numerology: Writers through-out history have often used numbers in their writings to signify things. The book of Revelation in the bible uses numbers to signify things. For example, Rev. 13:18 uses # 666 (and defines it as the number for the name of evil). Rev. Chapters 1 and 2; talk about 7-lamps, 7-churches, 7-stars.

We also notice that Moses (40-40-40) was 40 when he left Egypt to live in the desert, and 40 years later, he returns with his mission from God to free His People, and then Moses spends another 40 years in the desert as

God directs him to lead the Israelites through the desert – while God feeds them with both bread and quail falling from heaven daily – along with a portable rock, which gave them a portable water supply each day).

Seeing something 3-times is a good confirmation because tradition has shown that seeing anything once can be an accident, and seeing something twice may be a possibility, but seeing something 3-times is more convincing. Historically, Jewish traditions required two-or-three witnesses to make a firm and final decision. Three witnesses were best!

Here is what I have found reliable now for the past 40-years.

Look at some of the following scriptures to see how 3-witnesses were considered more reliable than 2-witnesses in scripture history:

- Deut.17 [6] On the evidence of two witnesses or of three witnesses he that is to die shall be put to death; a person shall not be put to death on the evidence of one witness.
- Deut.19 [15] "A single witness shall not prevail against a man for any crime or for any wrong in

connection with any offense that he has committed; only on the evidence of two witnesses, or of three witnesses, shall a charge be sustained.

- <u>Matt.18</u> [16] But if he does not listen, take one or two others along with you, that every word may be confirmed by the evidence of two or three witnesses.

- <u>2Cor.13</u> [1] This is the third time I am coming to you. Any charge must be sustained by the evidence of two or three witnesses.

- <u>1Tim.5</u> [19] Never admit any charge against an elder except on the evidence of two or three witnesses.

- <u>Heb.10</u> [28] A man who has violated the law of Moses dies without mercy at the testimony of two or three witnesses.

- <u>1John.5</u> [8] There are three witnesses, the Spirit, the water, and the blood; and these three agree.

Even the theory of "Statistical-Probability" has taught humans that if we flip a coin 100 times, we do typically get 50 heads and 50 tails, which means we would be very surprised to see anyone getting three heads when they flip a coin three times in a row. This is why seeing a number 7 or 77, in Christian Spirituality is not as convincing a clue until we see a 777 (which is more convincing – and which is "three witnesses of a # 7" (as in "777").

All outcomes of three numbers indicate good things ... except for # 666. And please note that if you see a mailbox or a car license plate which shows 666, it does not mean the owner is evil at all. After all, the number 666 is also just a number too (it comes before 667 and after 665 when we count numbers). So, seeing 666 does not always mean evil, but an author can often just use 666 in writing, in order <u>to indicate evil</u>.

If you (personally) use other meanings for the numbers below, then God will know your thoughts and intentions and He might use your meanings just for you (for your personal understanding). So, yes, you can use your own under-standing. However, the following are definitions which I have found being used ever since 1980, and I use them pretty successfully. I offer them to you here, just to help you to notice God's-Clues in your own life too.

I have found that once a person knows about the

following list God starts using it to give them clues. It is truly very amazing how many people begin to see and notice these clues – and just within days of learning about the following list and the following meaning of numbers. Simply stated, God can use anything and everything with which we are familiar in our lives (as ways for Him to show us clues of His love each day).

Here is the list that works best for most people I know:

- 111   Indicates   the Jewish   Holy   Prayer: "(Mark.12 [29] The Lord our God, the Lord is ONE (i.e. God is everywhere ... and there is only ONE-GOD)."

- 222 Jesus sent them (and us) out 2-By-2; so that He can (also) guide us and correct us -- from within the other person. It also signifies Jesus and each one of us united to Him ... "2 x 2" (that is; we each do co-exist with Jesus in us).

- 333 The Holy Trinity of God ... God has revealed Himself to us in history as three Divine Persons in one God (Father, Son, and Holy Spirit).

- 444 The holy name of: "The Blessed Virgin Mary, The Mother of Jesus."

- 555 Indicates Grace, which means: "The Holy Presence of God." (**)

- 666 The number for evil, as written in the Bible: - - as per the Book of Revelation – (Rev.13 verse-18).

- 777 The number signifying God's participation, permission or approval. See (*) below.

- 888 Indicates The Holy Name of Jesus.

- 999 Reflective of all of God's Tangible-Creation like Earth, Stars, Forests, Creatures, Laws of Nature, etc.

- 000 ... Signifies Eternity and Infinity.

Using the Alphabet --- as numbers as well:

You can also use the alphabet (to help with number clues). For example:

(A -- Is the first letter of the alphabet).

So you can use it, for a substitute for number 1).

(B – Is the second letter of the alphabet).

So you can use it, for a substitute for number 2).

(So you can use <u>C, for 3</u>, and <u>D for 4</u>, etc, etc. ...

<u>Therefore:</u> if you see D44 ... you can read it as 444.

if you see 55E ... you can read it as 555.

If you see EEE ... you can read it as 555.

If you see 77G ... you can read it as 777.

If you see GGG ... you can read it as 777.

.... Etcetera, Etcetera.

<u>For More Info</u> -- Google: "Catholic and Christian Numerology: 444, 555, and 777."

<u>NOTES</u>:

<u>(*) Re. 777...</u> Bethlehem where Jesus was born, and Golgotha, where Jesus died on a cross are both at 777 meters above sea level. God created Earth this way – as a clue that Jesus is truly God-Incarnate. Obviously, this was not created as a co-incidence!

You can Google: Bethlehem: 777 meters above sea level? ... and also ... Google: (Golgotha: 777 meters above sea level?) to prove these facts. Some references may vary by a couple of meters because of when the measurements were done or if there was construction around the site which may have added or deleted some of the earth around each space.

(**) **<u>Here is an interesting fact about (555):</u>** The Washington Monument in Washington, DC, was built to be 555 feet high. The number 555 signifies God's GRACE (God's Presence).

If you Google; "Height of Washington Monument in 1881," you will see that it was built to be 555 feet high. I would suggest that someone was trying to tell us in 1881 that "Our Nation Trusted in God." The currency we use is all stamped and noted "In God we trust." Let us pray that we in fact never forget that our nation's strength has always been the fact that we did trust in God's GRACE (God's Presence). Even our national anthem says ... "IN GOD WE TRUST." Please God, remind our politicians of this fact. Please!

Exhibit-B: FLEECING ... TO BE SURE WE ARE HEARING GOD CLEARLY

Bible Fleecing is a process which many saints in history have used when they wanted to be sure that they were doing God's-Will. Fleecing does come up as a topic in some chapters of this book, so a detailed explanation of it is shown below.

Often, when some biblical saints needed to be sure that they were clearly hearing God's will, they would ask God to show them some clues or signs to affirm that they were on the right track. As an example, some current saints might say today, "God, I will need you to supply the funds to pay for this task." And that can be a very convincing fleece!

Basically what happens when we use FLEECING is that we ask God to <u>please inspire us</u> with some clues to convince us that we are really hearing Him clearly. We do this when we have doubts, and God does not mind our being careful. And please note: we do not tell God what to do here. We just ask God to please help us to be sure we are not making a mistake in understanding His-Will about something.

Accordingly, when we ask God to inspire us with some fleecing-formula to convince us that we are really hearing Him correctly, He might inspire us to ONLY accept the plan and the steps which we are sensing that HE wants us to follow. But ONLY if something like one of the following (Fleece-Things) does happen first:

1. See if a (Red Cardinal Bird) lands in front of you within an hour.
2. Flip a coin to see if you get 3-heads ... when you flip it just 3-times. Note: The apostles drew LOTS to decide who was to become the replacement for Judas who had killed himself. (Ref. ACTS 1:24-26).
3. See if a specific best friend or relative actually calls you by 2 PM.
4. See if a yellow car passes you (in the next 5-minutes).
5. See if a car license plate of 555 or 777 (passes your car by noon).

God might inspire you with many other different methods, other than the 5-items shown above. The 5 items above are just a few of the ways which Jesus might inspire you to use; but God's list is larger than just 5 because God can do anything He wants to send us a clue. A little later in this exhibit, you will see several Bible passages listed where the saints in scriptures used fleeces to be sure they were doing God's Will.

The following is a very detailed explanation of Fleecing ... so that if you do ever need to discern something that is very heavy or risky in your life, like what General Gideon and many others have had to resolve, you might find some peace in the following process. If the following does not help you, then you might also look into the process of St. Ignatius of Loyola (the famous Jesuit saint) who is also famous for developing a process he outlines on "How to Discern Sprits and The Will of God." (You can Google: "St. Ignatius: for his discernment methods").

The following process is easier to follow and shorter in duration than the St. Ignatius method, and it does work out well for most people. So I have placed it here below to help you to have at least this method to use, just in case the other phases of talking to God (as explained in Chapter-02) are not working for you. If the following does not work well for you, then please look into the St. Ignatius methods cited above (or see your spiritual ministers, rabbis, and priests for more advice on how to discern God's Will).

Here are some DETAILED STEP-BY-STEP . . . SCRIPTURE FLEECING STEPS:

Sometimes God asks us to do things which require great risks and great faith or tremendous self-sacrifices. In General Gideon's case -- a classic case in the bible in Judges: Chapters #6 to #9) -- if he had not heard God correctly, he could be sending 32,000 soldiers to their death. (Ref. Judges: Chapter 7).

God always gives us what we need in these difficult and risky cases in order to correctly perceive His Will. Obviously, God, who knows all things, is not going to ask us to do things which we absolutely cannot do with His Help. What kind of a friend or coach or leader would ask their team to do things which the coach knows the team will fail at? God (the perfect coach) loves us with a love beyond measure and beyond human definition – and so He willingly helps us to be clear about what He wants us to do (whenever we honestly and respectfully ask God for clarity as Gideon and the other saints did do). They asked for clarity and God did give them the clarity to know His Will. The following referenced scripture from the New Testament shows that we do indeed receive some signs and clues from God to confirm our mission for God.

Mark.16:[20]   And they went forth and preached everywhere, while the Lord worked with them and confirmed the message by the signs that attended it.

Therefore when you see extreme risks of failure or inability on your part, you might want to ask God to help you by inspiring you with some fleecing-clues to make sure that you are not imagining things or being tempted. What we do in this case, is to respectfully ask Jesus to inspire our minds with some clues (like Gideon did with his FLEECES) so that we are sure we are hearing God's Will correctly and so we have a total deep peace about our choices. Jesus gives us a great heavenly peace (and certitude) when we are doing His Will.

For example; let's imagine that you think God has

asked you to sell your house and your car (<u>right now</u>) to someone you are currently meeting with for lunch at a restaurant -- and you think God is telling you to sell the car at a price of <u>only 20% of what you should charge</u> – and you also think God has asked you to call your spouse to pack up for a trip tonight because God wants you to travel with your spouse to <u>the other side of the world (for one week) to look for a place to live</u> and then to return back home in order to pack up and move to the other side of the world (immediately during the next 2-weeks).

This example may seem un-believable to you as you read this book today, but if you read about the things that God asked other saints in history (in scriptures below) ... you will see that the above is not so far-fetched when God is asking His great saintly people to do things for Him. Just consider the things that God asked St. Paul and St. Peter to do. And also consider St. Joan of Arc, St. Patrick, St. Thomas More, etc.

Since your-mission above seems very risky and unusual, you may want to be sure you are not being tempted, or you might want to be sure that you are NOT just imagining all this in your own mind. Therefore, you might ask God to PLEASE give you <u>some fleecing-clues</u> to help you to be sure that <u>you</u> are <u>hearing Him</u> correctly.

Jesus is not limited and can give you many different kinds of fleecing-clues and steps to follow when you ask, but let's just assume that He might inspire you and give you something like the following to help you to fleece in this example. The following is just one-possible example; Jesus will give you the right one to use when the time comes:

<u>Jesus might say:</u> "If in the next 10-minutes: (1). your spouse calls your cell phone within the next 5-minutes to just ask you <u>how you are doing</u> ... and then next; <u>your son also walks into the restaurant</u> which you are sitting in, before you finish talking to your wife ... and, next, it begins to rain outside, <u>then you will know</u> that I, Jesus, have told you to do what you are trying to verify."

At this point ... you did have some hard decisions to make like moving to the others side of the world, but Jesus just gave you some great amazing clues to look for (because if those amazing clues do actually happen, you will know that God did speak to you). And the reason you are sure that God did speak to you and give you those clues is simply and truly because YOU DID ASK GOD TO HELP YOU AND TO GIVE YOU CLUES TO FOLLOW. See, if you ask God for some clues to help you TO KNOW HIS WILL ... HE does absolutely answer you because HE does want you to know His Will. NOTE: We are positive from all of history that God loves us (EVERY ONE OF US), which is why He responds to all of our requests-for-help (to know His Will).

Sometimes, God will just nudge us to talk to 2 or 3 of our friends (separately and privately) to ask their separate advice and to take action only if they all agree with what you think God is telling you to do. This is an excellent reason why Jesus sent out His disciples (2 by 2) and why St. Paul came to visit with St. Peter in the bible twice -- when they both wanted to be sure they were doing God's Will. (Ref: Acts Chapter 15, and Galatians Chapter 1).

NOW, it is very important that you think carefully about the fleece-steps which God inspires for you to hear in your mind. This is important because you will need to ask God to change the fleece before you accept it (if there is something in the fleece which you happen to

<u>find "impossible for you to agree to").</u>

<u>I mean that</u>: Until you agree (100%) to follow the FLEECE steps which God has inspired into your mind for you, you really do not have an agreement or a fleece to follow with God yet. For example, James Chapter 1 in the bible says: "We can ask God for wisdom about anything, and God will answer – <u>but only if we ask without doubt.</u>" WE CAN'T BE INDECISIVE ABOUT IT AND DOUBTFUL ABOUT IT. WE HAVE TO BE CERTAIN THAT WE WILL DO WHAT GOD TELLS US TO DO FROM HIS FLEECE FORMULA OR WE SHOULD NOT ASK GOD TO GIVE US A FLEECE AT ALL. Therefore, if God asks you to follow a fleece which you think you cannot promise Him you will follow (because you have reasons which cause you to doubt), then ask God to please give you another **different fleece instead**, or ask God to give you some wisdom and clarity and courage to ultimately be able to promise Him your complete (100%) dedication to the fleece steps He gave you.

Do not worry about delaying your 100% promise to God. He is God and He wants to help us to have courage and to also be sure of His instructions and His Will. We can trust God to help us because He loves us. You will see many examples below of God helping other saints in the bible to be sure of God's will too.

So just be patient and wait for God to give you the courage and a total peace and certitude before you agree to any fleece. See the story of General Gideon for a good example of this by reading about General Gideon in Judges, Chapters: 6 to 9 in the bible. There are also many other bible examples below, which show how God does help people to be sure of His Will.

God will work with you to come up with the fleecing-steps which you can CONFIDENTLY ACCEPT AND AGREE TO. Because He wants us to seek His-Will in our lives, and He does not mind our being careful to hear Him correctly. God would rather have us careful and clear than to be reckless in doing things without talking to Him first for clarity. There is a lot of evidence of this in scriptures as well, as you will see below.

<u>Then finally; when you are firmly (100%) ready to promise Jesus that you will follow the fleece He has put into your mind</u> – then, you can proceed in faith to follow it and perform what God is asking you to do.

IMPORTANT: If the task you are going to perform is evil, or sinful, or illegal, or selfish; then you <u>must</u> <u>assume</u> it is not from God ... so then instead of fleecing you should visit your religious ministers and discuss it with them because scriptures say:

<u>1John.1</u> [5] this is the message we have heard from him and proclaim to you, that God is light and in him is no darkness at all.

<u>3 John.1</u> [11] Beloved, do not imitate evil but imitate good. He who does good is of God; he who does evil has not seen God.

God says in scriptures that He never creates evil. So, we NEVER consider doing anything evil, sinful, or illegal based on our own private fleece. God will honor our attempts to be sure we are hearing His Voice ... so there is absolutely no need to rush and make a serious error in doing God's will when you have doubts. The old adage is best which says: "<u>When in doubt, DON'T DO IT</u>."

There are many examples of places in the bible where people asked God to help them with Fleecing plans.

Many are shown below ... **but you do not need to read the following passages unless you want evidence of FLEECING cases in the bible**. I felt it necessary to give you all of the following items of evidence (from the Holy Bible) so that your faith can be strong and so that no one can mislead you about what the following scriptures say and imply. God Himself will help you to come up with a Fleece Plan whenever you need one, just as God did help the following people as well.

Gen.24 (Tony's note: Abraham sent his servant to go and find a wife for his beloved son Isaac) ..... [5] The servant said to him, "Perhaps the woman may not be willing to follow me to this land; must I then take your son back to the land from which you came?" [6] Abraham said to him, "See to it that you do not take my son back there. [7] The LORD, the God of heaven, who took me from my father's house and from the land of my birth, and who spoke to me and swore to me, `To your descendants I will give this land,' he will send his angel before you, and you shall take a wife for my son from there. [8] But if the woman is not willing to follow you, then you will be free from this oath of mine; only you must not take my son back there." [9] So the servant put his hand under the thigh of Abraham his master, and swore to him concerning this matter. [10] Then the servant took ten of his master's camels and departed, taking all sorts of choice gifts from his master; and he arose, and went to Mesopotamia, to the city of Nahor. [11] And he made the camels kneel down outside the city by the well of water at the time of evening, the time when women go out to draw water. [12] And he said, "O LORD, God of my master Abraham, grant me success today, I pray thee, and show steadfast love to my master Abraham. [13] Behold, I am standing by the spring of water, and the daughters of the men of the city are coming out to draw water. [14] Let the maiden to whom I shall say, `Pray let down your jar that I may drink,' and who shall say, `Drink, and I will water your camels' -- let her be the one whom thou hast appointed for thy servant Isaac. By this I shall know that thou hast shown steadfast love to my master." [15] Before he had done speaking, behold, Rebekah, who was born to Bethu'el the son of Milcah, the wife of Nahor, Abraham's brother, came out with her water jar upon her shoulder.

(Tony's Note: and Rebekah really did come out and do as the fleece specified above).

Judges 6: ... (Tony's Note ... The story of General Gideon is explained from chapter 6 to chapter 9 in the Book of Judges in the bible. And as indicted briefly above, this story clearly shows God allowing Gideon to ask for confirmations that Gideon is hearing God's inner voice correctly. General Gideon is being careful to be sure that he is hearing God correctly before sending 32,000 soldiers into battle). I urge you to read those chapters before you ask God for a difficult fleece plan because Gideon's story will help you to see that we can't agree to any fleece unless we do get it from God after we ask God for the fleece steps first, then firmly agree to the steps to follow. Finally, we need to have total peace (no fear or doubt), or we can't trust the fleece. God will give us peace if it is His Fleece.

2Kgs.20 ... (Tony's Note: God had told Hezekiah that he would live for another 15 years) .... [9] And Isaiah said, "This is the sign to you from the LORD, that the LORD will do the thing that he has promised: shall the shadow go forward ten steps, or go back ten steps?" [10] And Hezeki'ah answered, "It is an easy thing for the shadow to lengthen ten steps; rather let the shadow go back ten steps." [11] And Isaiah the prophet cried to the LORD; and he brought the shadow back ten steps, by which the sun had declined on the dial of Ahaz.

(Tony's note: Therefore Hezekiah's Fleece request – which was offered by God through the prophet Isaiah – was indeed gladly answered by God to help Hezekiah to be sure of God's voice).

Isa.7 (Tony's Note: God WILLINGLY gave Ahaz the opportunity to ask for a fleece sign from God, but Ahaz was so obstinate that he would not even bother to do so) .... [10] Again the LORD spoke to Ahaz, [11] "Ask a sign of the LORD your God; let it be deep as Sheol or high as heaven." [12] But Ahaz said, "I will not ask, and I will not put the LORD to the test." [13] And Isaiah said, "Hear then, O house of David! Is it too little for you to weary men, that you weary my God also? [14] Therefore the Lord himself will give you a sign. Behold, a young woman shall conceive and bear a son, and shall call his name Immanuel.

(Tony note: The above clue-sign from God was later achieved in the birth of Jesus, born unto us through to The Blessed Virgin Mary).

Matt.17 ... (Tony's Note: Jesus uses a miracle to show Peter a clue-sign that he must pay the taxes) ... [24]

When they came to Caper'na-um, the collectors of the half-shekel tax went up to Peter and said, "Does not your teacher pay the tax?" [25] He said, "Yes." And when he came home, Jesus spoke to him first, saying, "What do you think, Simon? From whom do kings of the earth take toll or tribute; from their sons or from others?" [26] And when he said, "From others," Jesus said to him, "Then the sons are free. [27] However, not to give offense to them, go to the sea and cast a hook, and take the first fish that comes up, and when you open its mouth you will find a shekel; take that and give it to them for me and for yourself."

(Tony Note: In that case; Jesus gave Simon-Peter a clue-sign even before St. Peter asked).

Mark.14 ... (Tony's Note: Jesus sends two disciples to prepare the upper room for the Passover feast) ... [12] And on the first day of Unleavened Bread, when they sacrificed the Passover lamb, his disciples said to him, "Where will you have us go and prepare for you to eat the Passover?" [13] And he sent two of his disciples, and said to them, "Go into the city, and a man carrying a jar of water will meet you; follow him, [14] and wherever he enters, say to the householder, `The Teacher says,

Where is my guest room, where I am to eat the Passover with my disciples?' [15] And he will show you a large upper room furnished and ready; there prepare for us." [16] And the disciples set out and went to the city, and found it as he had told them; and they prepared the Passover.

Luke.19 ... (Tony's Note: Jesus sent his disciples to borrow a colt) ... [29] When he drew near to Beth'phage and Bethany, at the mount that is called Olivet, he sent two of the disciples, [30] saying, "Go into the village opposite, where on entering you will find a colt tied, on which no one has ever yet sat; untie it and bring it here. [31] If anyone asks you, `Why are you untying it?' you shall say this, `The Lord has need of it.'" [32] So those who were sent went away and found it as he had told them.

Acts.1 ... (Tony's Note: The apostles chose lots to replace Judas who betrayed Jesus) ... [24] And they prayed and said, "Lord, who knowest the hearts of all men, show which one of these two thou hast chosen [25] to take the place in this ministry and apostleship from which Judas turned aside, to go to his own place." [26] And they cast lots for them, and the lot fell on <u>Matthias;</u> and he was enrolled with the eleven apostles.

OTHER (POSSIBLE) BIBLE FLEECINGS: The following items are listed for your discernment as additional possible cases where fleecing was involved as well.

Genesis: Ch.15:7-8 [7] And he said to him, "I am the LORD who brought you from Ur of the Chalde'ans, <u>to give you this land to possess.</u>" [8] But Abram said, "O Lord GOD, <u>how am I to know that I shall possess it</u>?

Genesis: 18:3-14 [3] and Abraham said, "My lord, <u>if I have found favor in your sight</u>, do not pass by your servant. [4] Let a little water be brought, and wash your feet, and rest yourselves under the tree, [5] while I fetch a morsel of bread, that you may refresh yourselves, and after that you may pass on -- since you have come to your servant." So they said, "Do as you have said." [6] And Abraham hastened into the tent to Sarah, and said, "Make ready quickly three measures of fine meal, knead it, and make cakes." [7] And Abraham ran to the herd, and took a calf, tender and good, and gave it to the servant, who hastened to prepare it. [8] Then he took curds, and milk, and the calf which he had prepared, and set it before them; and he stood by them under the tree while they ate. [9] They said to him, "Where is Sarah your wife?" And he said, "She is in the tent." [10] The LORD said, "<u>I will surely return to you in the spring, and Sarah your wife shall have a son.</u>" And Sarah was listening at the tent door behind him. [11] Now Abraham and Sarah were old, advanced in age; it had ceased to be with Sarah after the manner of women. [12] So Sarah laughed to herself, saying, "After I have grown old, and my husband is old, shall I have pleasure?" [13] The LORD said to Abraham, "Why did Sarah laugh, and say, `Shall I indeed bear a child, now that I am old?' [14] Is anything too hard for the LORD? At the appointed time I will return to you, <u>in the spring, and Sarah shall have a son.</u>"

Genesis: 18:26-32 [26] And the LORD said, "If I find at Sodom fifty righteous in the city, I will spare the whole place for their sake." [27] Abraham answered, "Behold, I have taken upon myself to speak to the Lord, I who am but dust and ashes. [28] <u>Suppose five of the fifty righteous are lacking? Wilt thou destroy the whole city for lack of five?</u>" And he said, "I will not destroy it if I find forty-five there." [29] Again he spoke to him, and said, "Suppose forty are found there." He answered,

"For the sake of forty I will not do it." [30] Then he said, "Oh let not the Lord be angry, and I will speak. Suppose thirty are found there." He answered, "I will not do it, if I find thirty there." [31] He said, "Behold, I have taken upon myself to speak to the Lord. Suppose twenty are found there." He answered, "For the sake of twenty I will not destroy it." [32] Then he said, <u>"Oh let not the Lord be angry, and I will speak again</u> but this once. <u>Suppose ten are found there." He answered, "For the sake of ten I will not destroy it."</u>

Matthew 16:15-19 [15] Jesus said to them, <u>"But who do you say that I am?"</u>

[16] Simon Peter replied, "You are the Christ, the Son of the living God." [17] And Jesus answered him, <u>"Blessed are you, Simon Bar-Jona! Flesh and blood has not revealed this to you, but my Father who is in heaven.</u> [18] And I tell you, you are Peter, and <u>on this rock I will build my church</u>, and the powers of death shall not prevail against it. [19] I will give you the keys of the kingdom of heaven, and whatever you bind on earth shall be bound in heaven, and whatever you loose on earth shall be loosed in heaven."

WOW – how great is our God! Just precisely as I typed the number above (as in Genesis: 18:3, 14 above), the TV announcer on the TBN-TV network was speaking and co-incidentally recited "that exact same passage in scripture". And, the announcer did speak each number – and exactly as my fingers were striking each of the 7-Keys (18:3-14).

Jesus was actually allowing my fingers to be striking the exact-keys <u>in unison</u> with the TV-person-speaker, who was actually saying each number as I hit each key.

I guess some people might call this a "surreal-experience," but I am positive that it was another wonderful Co-incidence-miracle from Jesus! I truly felt Jesus present at that moment, almost as if He had taken control of my hands and fingers (as if my hands were His gloves for a moment) and He was striking the keys as He was speaking through the person on the TV. Thank you, dear Jesus, for your abundant love and many blessings!

<u>PLEASE REMEMBER:</u> Take time to be sure that you will do what Jesus has inspired <u>in your mind as a fleece ... before you promise Jesus to follow the fleece.</u> The

reason for this care at the beginning is because after you state the fleece plan, the devil may try to cause you a lot of doubts and anxiety unless you are positive and comfortable and committed to follow the fleece beforehand. The devil likes to confuse us and cause us doubts when we are talking to God. So, be sure you will follow the fleece (before you begin to wait for the fleece to happen).

Exhibit-C: *A FREE VIDEO ON HOW TO HAVE CONVERSATIONS WITH GOD EACH DAY.*

--- This video explains how to Listen to and have conversations with God (like Moses and the saints did).

It really is not very complicated (because God Himself wants to talk to each one of us all the time). God made us to become His friends and He is always with us everywhere. He waits for us to talk to Him.

If you type the following lines into your Google or Internet searches ... you will be able to see the VIDEO on You-tube. (There are three parts to watch, one at a time):

J bomb, you tube, Tony Coscia, listening to God – part 1

J bomb, you tube, Tony Coscia, listening to God – part 2

J bomb, you tube, Tony Coscia, listening to God – part 3

If the above do not work ... then try the following instead:

YouTube, 2017, Tony Coscia, conversations with God-part1

YouTube, 2017, Tony Coscia, conversations with God-part2

YouTube, 2017, Tony Coscia, conversations with God-part3

Exhibit-D: (Page-1) How to Order Miraculous Medals:

I purchase these medals (part number i-086), which are all delivered and individually packaged inside of individual envelopes, which also include a small card that explains what the Miraculous Medal is all about.

I typically fold two envelopes together -- and slide them both into the driver's side (circular-door-handles of cars) as I am walking to or from my car in shopping malls. It is easy to do this as I walk past the cars I see as I am entering the mall. I also do this again as I leave the mall (figuring that God has gotten the people He wished to come and park next to me while I was shopping inside).

I order these medals from The Association of The Miraculous Medal at 1811 West St. Joseph Street, Perryville, MO 63775-1598 ... Phone: 1-800-264-6279.

I normally order two types of medals:

1-- A Silver Colored Medal and info card neatly placed into envelopes – part number – **i-086**.

2 – A Gold Colored Medal, loose in bulk form; to hand out to people I meet – part number – **m-006**.

These medals are all aluminum and are very reasonably priced as of this typing in the year 2017 (at from 8 cents to 15 cents per medal).

A book by a Catholic Priest ... for your info:

77 Stories of the Miraculous Medal (English), Author: Pfarrer Karl Maria Harrer

The author, the German Priest Fr. Karl Maria Harrer, has collected 77 true stories about the Miraculous Medal for several decades now. The stories show us how the Virgin Mary, who appeared in Paris in 1830 to a French Sister Katharina Labouré, supports us in our daily life. Therefore, the Medal of the Immaculate Conception has become a very popular vessel of grace and is truly miraculous. That is why it is often called: "The Miraculous Medal."

<u>Exhibit-E: God's Affirmations and Confirmations of this book:</u>

<u>**An affirmation**</u> is when something or someone agrees with a point being made ... and ... <u>**A confirmation**</u> is when clear evidence can be shown that a thing has also happened to someone else, or for a second or third time. So, a Confirmation can often produce and create a FACT. There are both AFFIRMATIONS and CONFIRMATIONS in what follows below:

The following items are things which happened in my life (while I was writing this book) ... which brought me great joy and great peace, and which showed me that God was participating with me in the process of writing this book.

Can you imagine my joy in seeing that God was really typing along with me every day? First, I had to get over the shock of realizing that God was really that close to me as I was typing and thinking of what to write, but I realized how fortunate I was to be given this positive proof. I know I am just a speck of dust in the whole universe (I am very aware of that). However, from this point onward, I am ALSO aware that God Almighty loved me so much that He actually showed me that He was typing along with me in producing this book. Some of the evidence of this, which God is allowing me to share, follows below:

The following items were often also cited in various pages as you were reading this book ... and the book then often directed you to this page for this info (the book gave you the reference item number below as a reference point to match the item you were reading about at the time).

1. **There are no Co-incidences:** Cardinal Dolan of New York was on EWTN-TV (on 05-15-2017 as I was typing this book), and he stated that it was true that Pope John Paul II and President Ronald Reagan were both very good friends (especially after they were both almost assassinated within 7-weeks of each other) and both of them agreed that there were no co-incidences where God is concerned (most co-incidences are really ACTS OF GOD -- "MIRACLES").

Both of these friends had assassination attempts on their lives in the same 7-week period. March 30, 1981, was the Reagan assignation attempt ... and ... May 13, 1981 (The feast day of Our Lady of Fatima), was the Pope's assassination attempt. They both knew that it was miracles that kept them alive for the bigger things they both achieved after they both survived the attacks.

<u>The above therefore confirms what this book is about ...</u> namely that when we are devoted to and attentive to God and trying to be His friend, Co-incidences are really miracles from God.

2. **<u>Tiny Miracles</u>:** Father Spitzer, on his EWTN-TV show about the UNIVERSE, which aired at 1:00:am on 05-20-2017, as I was typing this exact point into this book explained that "[w]hen we see God actually intervening and acting miraculously in the very tiny (and the tiniest) events in our lives – it serves to build up our faith and trust and love of God more-quickly and more strongly because we come to realize how God is actually stooping down to the tiniest of levels in our lives to move

things miraculously for us (even in what seems to some people to look like a coincidence)."

This then confirmed the book while I was typing it. Wherein I was inspired by Jesus to explain how often God comes and joins us in the very minutia of our lives, because He can, and because He loves us.

There was another similar miracle like the above with Father Spitzer which is mentioned in the "About the Author" section of this book.

3. Confirmed – precisely as I was typing: Often as I was typing edits to this book, I would hear someone on TV or RADIO or in the room with me speak the exact word I was using to replace a word being replaced. This happened no less than 15-times in just one-week (and I guess you either had to be there with me ... or trust me). It really did happen – Thank You Jesus!

For example, Jesus asked me to edit and say that: (the weekly With-777 letters are sent out for FREE ... and just precisely as I typed the word FREE – a radio announcer was advertising something and said ("remember: it is free") ... saying FREE exactly and simultaneously ... as I began to type the word "FREE." (God naturally timed this precision-miracle)!

In addition, on the previous day before the above FREE miracle, Jesus inspired me to PATCH a paragraph in one of the stories in this book to make it clearer. I did not want to re-write it so I was not happy. Then Jesus gently inspired me again saying lovingly in my soul and gently ("it is not clear enough ... you have to patch it") ... and the Radio announcer said the word PATCH exactly at the same second as Jesus also said that word PATCH in my soul. It was like hearing it in stereo! And I sensed Jesus smiling as He said, "Yes; I did orchestrate that confirmation of My Voice for you just then Tony."

4. **God calls us all by name:** (The following item refers to the "About the Author" section of this book): 20-years after having picked the name John as my confirmation name, I, Tony, was inspired by Jesus to notice that the feast days of my 3-patron-saints: (Anthony, Francis, and John)

are exactly 7-days apart each year in January –
(respectively on 1-17-XX, 1-24-XX, and 1-31-XX,
every year). Three weeks at 7-days apart is
commemorative of the holy number of 777 (and
777 historically indicates God's approval). The
fact that Jesus suddenly nudged me to notice this
one day is one of those co-incidence-miracles
which bring all of us joy in being a Friend of God!

Everyone should check the dates of their patron
saint feast days to see if there are some Co-
incidence-Clue-Miracles in the dates.

In addition, every single year for well over the
past 20 years, I was reminded by my calendar on
January 17, 24, and 31 that Jesus convinced me
that my name was not just a co-incidence.

When I finally did read the lives of these three
saints, I found that I have been doing many of the
same things which these saints did do in their
own daily lives too. This is not uncommon in the
Catholic Faith because the names we choose for
our children do honor the saint whom we chose as
the child's namesake. Choosing a saint's name

also brings with it the positive aid and assistance of that saint from heaven to help the people who have been named with the saint's name

We usually pick a child's name in memory of the saint's holy life and the saint's walk in life with Jesus among us. And we do this so our child will have the special help of that saint during our child's lifetime (something like a guardian angel).

When we take a saint's name as our name (we call them our patron saints because we are hoping for their protections and their spiritual guidance in life). In my case, it turned out that all 3 saint-names which I had been given in life (all line up 7-days apart every January) beginning with January 17 each year.

I did not realize until Jesus showed me that; I had wound up walking down the same pathways in life as the three saints I was named after — as indicated below:

For example: St. Anthony of Padua was a preacher and an evangelist just like I had also become in life, even before I knew this fact about

279

St. Anthony of Padua. Then I also realized that <u>St. Francis De Sales</u> also sent out letters like The W.I.T.H- Letters which I have also been mailing out since 1980. And, <u>St. Francis de Sales</u> is called the patron saint of Journalists and Writers, and I have been writing With-Letters since 1980 and am now led to write this book as well. Finally, <u>St. John Bosco</u> was also a Sunday School Teacher just as I have also been now for over 40-years.

To appreciate the above co-incidence-Miracles (namely, that my pursuits in life have paralleled those of the saints I am named after), we do have to realize and appreciate that I began to follow all of those life choices above in my own life – which we only now can see (in hindsight) as matching the talents and life choices of all three of my saint-namesakes. I had no idea I was following a pre-planned pathway which God had arranged for me, ever since my name became Anthony, Francis, John (after my Confirmation in the year 1952, 65 years ago)!

Just before finishing this book, I found out that I made my first communion on 05-21-1950, one day before the Feast Day of St. Rita of Cascia (a favorite saint of my family). The feast day of 05-21 commemorates a Martyr (St. Cristobal Magallanes who was martyred because he was defending the practice of the perpetuating the daily reception of Holy Communion at mass).

Also please notice these two bible passages:

Ref. -- Bible passage: Isaiah 43: [1] <u>I have called you by name</u>, you are mine.

Ref. – Bible passage: John.10 ... Jesus said ... [1] "Truly, truly, I say to you, he who does not enter the sheepfold by the door but climbs in by another way, that man is a thief and a robber; [2] but he who enters by the door is the shepherd of the sheep. [3] To him the gatekeeper opens; the sheep hear his voice, <u>and he calls his own sheep by name</u> and leads them out. [4] When he has brought out all his own, he goes before them, and the sheep follow him, for they know his voice.

5. **Client Box Story-02:** When you read this miracle story, you will notice that Jesus led me to meet the exact client mentioned in the story (again, by a Godly Coincident-Miracle) on the very day that I had typed this miracle story into this book. And noticeably this was an important miracle because the client explained that she had 70-boxes to check not the 17-boxes which I thought she had told me about earlier. So co-incidentally meeting her (on the day that I typed her miracle as 17-boxes) was indeed a miracle from God. It got me to change the book from 17 boxes to say 70 boxes instead. If I did not accidentally meet her, the book would have been incorrect, so I see this as God participating very closely with me to produce this book in line with His Will.

This was a definite Godly Confirmation: Imagine typing something from memory and then, an hour later, actually seeing the same person whom you just typed about ... telling you and confirming to you what you had just typed needed a revision!

6. **If you refer to the miracle in Chapter 05** about "My Wonderful Wife Julie (passed away after 53 years of marriage)", you will find an amazing confirmation that occurred as I was

typing this book ... precisely to the moment as I was typing that particular miracle. This is one case where it is hardly possible to imagine anyone doubting that God does send us Co-incidence-Miracles when we are trying to do His will.

<u>The Baltimore catechism is famous for stating:</u> "God made us to Know Him, Love Him, and to Serve Him."

<u>Furthermore; St. John tells us in scriptures ... 1 John.4</u>

[7] Beloved, let us love one another; for love is of God, and he who loves is born of God and knows God. [8] He who does not love does not know God; for God is love. [10] In this is love, not that we loved God but that he loved us and sent his Son to be the expiation for our sins. [11] Beloved, if God so loved us, we also ought to love one another. . [15] Whoever confesses that Jesus is the Son of God, God abides in him, and he in God. ... **[19] We love, because he first loved us.**

<u>7. Just as I finished typing the pages</u> about the miracle called: "A Job -- In the Nick-Of-Time" (in chapter 07), I was nudged to edit and add a note to say "That God really unbelievably and unconditionally -- loves each one of us;" I heard an evangelist on the TBN Television network speaking (because the TV was already turned on while I was typing).

And, just as I typed the edited words into that page of this book, I heard the evangelist say: "God loves us with a love beyond our understanding; because as the Bibles says: **God is Love!**"

So, this was another perfectly timed clue (coincidence Miracle) from God that He wanted this book to be worded the way He had just nudged me to edit it.

Thank You Jesus, for your constant help and for all of your clues Lord!

The following items (# 8 # 9, and # 10) were taken from Exhibit-B because while I was typing Exhibit-B items, Jesus sent the following AFFRMATIONS that He was helping me to write this book. I thought you might appreciate seeing this blessing as another example of God's many varieties of Co-incidence-miracles" which were still happening as we were assembling this book for publication.

8. (At the end of this section in Exhibit B ... I noted how the TV speaker was saying exactly what I was typing – in unison as I was typing each key).

I felt as if my hands were just gloves, and Jesus was wearing my hands during that coincidence-miracle.

9. On 6/30/2017 as was driving home after Saturday morning mass ... I heard that a musical band had just released their new song called "444" .... And then I noticed that I was following a car with the license plate number 888.

When I got home, I began to edit this book again from where I left off on Friday night. And I noticed that the next page I needed to start editing on this Saturday morning was the Miracle Story which is labeled: "Store Shopping (team 444) with (An 888-Buddy)"!

10. The following is taken from Exhibit-B and it was stated on the last page of Exhibit-B. You can look at Exhibit-B for more clarification of the following summary if necessary.

WOW – how great is our God! Just precisely as I typed the number above as in (Genesis: 18:3, 14 above), the

TV announcer on the TBN-TV network was speaking and (co-incidentally recited "that exact same passage in scripture"). And, the announcer did speak each number – and exactly as my fingers were striking each of the 7-Keys: (18:3-14).

Jesus was actually allowing my fingers to be striking the exact-keys in unison with the TV-person-speaker, who was actually saying each number as I hit each key.

I guess some people might call this a "surreal-experience," but I am positive that it was another wonderful Co-incidence-miracle from Jesus! I truly felt Jesus present at that moment, almost as if He had taken control of my hands and fingers (as if my hands were His gloves for a moment) and He was striking the keys as He was speaking through the person on the TV. Thank you dear Jesus for your abundant love and many blessings!

11. Godly Confirmation (by the movie about a SPELLING BEE):

After the book was given to the publisher, I sat down to watch a TV movie that I had recorded several days earlier. I was having my doubts about the book and whether or not I was good enough to actually do such a thing as write a book about God and His Miracles. I know many more-capable people than I who could have done a great job writing the book instead of me.

And I also had second thoughts about the title that I was already inspired to use many months ago as -- "Tony's 50,000 Co-incidence Miracles."

But it was too late now to be doubting that I was good enough or if the title was great or not because I had already discussed all of this with Jesus long before this day and although I can't immediately recall every word that Jesus gave me (I do know that Jesus did get me through all of my doubts for the past 12 months). Now that I had submitted the final book to the publisher, there was no sense thinking about am I good enough or is the title a good title to use.

Well (Thank You Jesus) ... because at 41 minutes into this 2 hour movie, a student is asked by her teacher to read the plaque on the wall and to read it out loud to him.

She reads it and it says all that I needed to hear ... in part it said things like the following:

"Who are you to think that you are not good enough now, especially after you can see all of the gifts and talents which were given to you? And how do you dare even think to not stand up and show forth the talent and ability which you were gifted with ... so that others might notice and benefit from the example which you will set before them?"

..... And then, even while I was still stunned and excited about the great Godly confirmation (and co-incidence miracle) which I just heard; another amazing thing happened:

..... At 1-hour and 13 minutes into the movie (the student's mother tells her self-doubting child, who is feeling un-worthy) that she does indeed now stand out as a very qualified and exceptionally talented student -- and therefore, "From now on, she will probably find that she has 50,000 tutors coming to her to ask her to please let me tutor you."

And right after this moment in the movie, the movie then shows several people coming to tutor the young lady. And each time a tutor tries to tutor her, she has a flash-back that reminds her of what her mother had said

("From now on, you will probably find 50,000 tutors coming to want to tutor you now").

For me, as I was watching this movie, every time I heard them say 50,000 tutors in the movie, Jesus spoke into my heart reminding me that He had given me that title to use for this book: *Tony's 50,000 Co-incidence Miracles.*

Thank You Jesus, for teaching me that the co-incidence miracles which you do send to us in our lives are like many tutoring steps which you send to us during the day. Your miracles are often ways for you to teach and TUTOR us in many things.

The movie was released to the public in 2006 which was 11 years before I wrote the book. So the movie was just waiting for me for 11-years to notice both the plaque message in the movie and to notice the term that 50,000 tutors would come to teach that student (just as Jesus had sent me 50,000 tutors -- in the form of co-incidence miracles -- for the past 50 years, to teach me and prepare me for many things).

The title to the 2006 movie was: "AKEELA AND THE BEE". The key actor was Laurence Fishburne. The key actress was Angela Bassett. The credits showed the producers to be Lions Gate 2929, Cinema Gypsy, and Starbucks Entertainment.

12. NOTE: Please also see Exhibit-H for a very important Confirmation from God and The Blessed Virgin Mary at Medjugorje on 08-02-2017.

13. NOTE: Please also see the Summary and Conclusion Statement (for the post script at the end of Chapter 9) in order to see another amazing confirmation from Jesus (in the very final moments before printing). That final confirmation of many was sent by Jesus to let us know that He was pleased with this book and with its intended mission. How wonderful Jesus is to us -- that in the very final moments of concluding this book; He lovingly sends us a miracle to tell us He is pleased with this book and with its mission. Thank You Jesus!

Exhibit-F: Ideas on how to use this book for groups and clubs and for discussions with family and friends:

1. **Family** – each family member can read one miracle-story per chapter and then share their own understanding and summary of that story at Sunday meal time, so that everyone reads a different story for each week.

2. **Workplace** – similar to the Family idea above, co-workers can do something similar once a week at a weekly breakfast or luncheon meeting.

3. **Many others** -- like item 1 and 2 above. LIKE: school classes, or organizations which meet monthly or weekly ... who may want to consider the topic of: "Was it a Miracle or Not" ... as they discuss things that are happening each week in their own lives too.

4. **School Plays or TV or Movie:** Imagine creating movies or school plays based on true stories about God's Miracles. This would help movie-goers to realize that they do receive

miracles every day. I am thinking of how the movie with Jimmy Stewart called *It's A Wonderful Life* had a great effect on showing people how precious life really is.

Virgin Mary – Medjugorje
Courtesy of Wikimedia

Exhibit-G: -- Catechism references:

As a friend of Jesus, we become mindful of God being present and living near us and with us during our normal daily activities. We experience some close communication with God as well. God nudges and prompts us to do good and not evil during our daily walk with God.

<u>The Catholic Catechism explains that we have the AMAZING benefit of "The Voice of God in Our Conscience" all day long, as follows:</u>

1776 -- Deep within his conscience man discovers a law which he has not laid upon himself but which he must obey. Its voice, ever calling him to love and to do what is good and to avoid evil, sounds in his heart at the right moment. ... For man has in his heart a law inscribed by God. ... His conscience is man's most secret core and his sanctuary. **There he is alone with God** whose voice echoes in his depths."47

1777 -- Moral conscience,48 present at the heart of the person, enjoins him at the appropriate moment to do good and to avoid evil. It also judges particular choices, approving those that are good and denouncing those that are evil.49 It bears witness to the authority of truth in reference to the supreme Good to which the human person is drawn, and it welcomes the commandments. When he listens to his conscience, **the prudent man can hear God speaking**.

1778 -- Conscience is a judgment of reason whereby the human person recognizes the moral quality of a concrete act that he is going to perform, is in the process of performing, or has already completed. In all he says and does, man is obliged to follow faithfully what he knows to be just and right. It is by the judgment of his conscience that man perceives and recognizes the prescriptions of the divine law:

Conscience is a law of the mind; yet [Christians] would not grant that it is nothing more; I mean that it was not a dictate, nor conveyed the notion of responsibility, of duty, of a grace, speaks to us behind a veil, and teaches and rules us by his representatives. **Conscience is the aboriginal Vicar of Christ.**

1779 -- It is important for every person to be sufficiently present to himself in order to hear and **follow the voice of his conscience**. This requirement of interiority is all the more necessary as life often distracts us from any reflection, self-examination or introspection: Return to your conscience, question it. . . . Turn inward, brethren, and in everything you do, **see God as your witness**.

Jesus Christ from Hagia Sophia
Courtesy of Wikipedia

Exhibit-H: -- Medjugorje 08-02-2017
CONFIRMATION of this book:

On August 2, 2017, two days after this book was finished and already sent to the publisher on 07-31-2017; the following message was received from The Blessed Virgin Mary in Medjugorje (Yugoslavia). Tony has underlined the statements below which do confirm the inspired mission he was given for this book entitled: **"Tony's 50,000 Co-incidence Miracles."**

Today, August 2nd, 2017, Our Lady appeared to the visionary Mirjana Soldo and delivered the following message:

"Dear children,

According to the will of the Heavenly Father, as the mother of Him who loves you, I am here with you to help you to come to know Him and to follow Him. My

Son has left you His foot-prints to make it easier for you to follow Him. Do not be afraid. Do not be uncertain, I am with you. Do not permit yourselves to be discouraged because much prayer and sacrifice are necessary for those who do not pray, do not love and do not know my Son. You help, by seeing your brothers in them. Apostles of my love, harken to my voice within you, feel my motherly love. Therefore pray, pray by doing, pray by giving, pray with love, pray in work and thoughts, in the name of my Son. All the more love that you give, so much more of it you will also receive. Love which emanates from love illuminates the world. Redemption is love, and love has no end. When my Son comes to the earth anew, He will look for love in your hearts. My children, many are the acts of love which He has done for you. I am teaching you to see them, to comprehend them and to thank Him by loving Him and always anew forgiving your neighbors. Because to love my Son means to forgive. My Son is not loved if the neighbor cannot be forgiven, if there is not an effort to comprehend the neighbor, if he is judged. My children, of what use is your prayer if you do not love and forgive? Thank you."

Please ALSO refer to pages 235-238 for an affirmation (by Jesus), which reads in part as follows:

I opened the book called *THE IMITATION OF CHRIST* written in 1391, and 100 years before Christopher Columbus discovered America. I wound up opening it at random to the section marked in the book as <u>BOOK III (chapter one)</u> -- and I read these words:

"Blessed is that man who hears Jesus speaking in his soul, and who takes from His mouth some word of comfort. Blessed are those ears which hear the secret whisperings of Jesus."

Next, Jesus nudged and inspired me to take the book called "HE AND I" (volume 1). I opened it at random and wound up seeing the last two paragraphs of the entry which was made in that book as dated January 3, 1948. Here is what Jesus said to Gabrielle Bossis in those two paragraphs (and what Jesus was now also saying to me – after writing this book with and for Him):

"You see, what pains MY love is indifference, apathy, stagnation. When it comes to ME, many people act as if

I was still dead. But MY child, I am alive and I am near them, in them, waiting for them to talk to ME. I am waiting for their hearts to beat a little for ME.

I require so little, am so readily pleased. I only ask to be invited and I look after the banquet."

Well, as you probably noticed already by now, the mission and purpose of this book was precisely to have people do exactly what Jesus just told me in the above two paragraphs. This then is the last of many co-incidence-miracles which we have received while writing this book (see Exhibit-E for others).

(For a public domain version of Thomas à Kempis's book *The Imitation of Christ*, see http://www.catholicplanet.com/ebooks/Imitati on-of-Christ.pdf)

<u>Exhibit I – The Marble Slab Miracle</u>

Please notice that you may see nothing when you stare into the marble slab below, but on the next second page, the intricate detail and matching sizes for the faces and eyes of both Blessed Mary and St. Joseph (are perfectly scaled to size). And you can also notice the Christ child on Mary's lap, and the form of the donkey as well).

An "Ordinary" Marble Slab

An "Extraordinary" Image Emerges